# Introduction to Angel Investing

Angel 101 and Angel 201

Student Edition

# Books by the Authors

**Fundamentals of Angel Investing**
A Guide to the Principles, Skills and Concepts Every Angel Investor Needs to Succeed

**Angel Investing by the Numbers**
Valuation, Capitalization, Portfolio Construction and Startup Economics

**Leaders Wanted: Making Startup Deals Happen**
Advanced Techniques in Deal Leadership and Due Diligence for Early Stage Investors

**Guide, Advise and Inspire: How Startup Boards Drive Growth and Exits**
An Overview of the Principles, Skills and Concepts Every Early Stage Company Board Member Needs to Succeed

**Venture Capital: A Practical Guide**
A Guide to Fund Formation and Management

# Angel Investing Course Books by the Authors

**Angel 101 and Angel 201**
Introduction to Angel Investing

**Due Diligence**
Evaluating Investment Opportunities

**Termsheets and Valuations**
Negotiating Investments

**Portfolio Success and Startup Economics**
Angel Finance

# Introduction to Angel Investing

Angel 101 and Angel 201

# Student Edition

Hambleton Lord

Christopher Mirabile

Seraf
Compass
Publications

www.seraf-investor.com

Copyright © 2018 by Seraf LLC

All rights reserved. No part of this publication may be reproduced, distributed, or transmitted in any form or by any means, including photocopying, recording, or other electronic or mechanical methods, without the prior written permission of the publisher, except in the case of brief quotations embodied in critical reviews and certain other noncommercial uses permitted by copyright law. For permission requests, contact the publisher, addressed "Attention: Permissions Coordinator," at the address below.

support@seraf-investor.com

www.seraf-investor.com


Cover Illustration Copyright: lublubachka / 123RF Stock Photo

# Table of Contents

1. **Introduction to Angel Investing**   1

2. **Angel 101**   5
   - 2.1. Introduction   9
   - 2.2. Getting Started   11
   - 2.3. Portfolio Theory   14
   - 2.4. Investment Process   21
   - 2.5. Deal Flow   27
   - 2.6. Due Diligence   31
   - 2.7. Angel Roles   41
   - 2.8. Angel 101 Resources   45

3. **Angel 201**   53
   - 3.1. Introduction   57
   - 3.2. Termsheets   59
   - 3.3. Capitalization Tables   65
   - 3.4. Valuations   73
   - 3.5. Follow-On Theory   83
   - 3.6. Types of Exits   87
   - 3.7. Angels and Taxes   93
   - 3.8. Angel 201 Resources   97

# Appendix

I. Overview   105

II. Early Stage Investment Portfolio Modeling Tool   109

III. Due Diligence Report Template   113

IV. Due Diligence Checklist   123

V. Customer Reference Check Questionnaire   131

VI. Management Assessment Questionnaire   135

VII. Guidelines for Successful Board Meetings   139

VIII. Deal Terms Expectations Summary Memo   145

IX. A Guide to Angel Investing Docs: Preferred Stock Deal   153

X. A Guide to Angel Investing Docs: Convertible Debt Deal   163

XI. Sample Termsheet: Preferred Stock   169

XII. Sample Termsheet: Convertible Note   173

XIII. Valuation Modeling Tool   179

XIV. Capitalization Tables with Waterfall Analysis   189

XV. Exit Planning Guide   197

# Introduction to Angel Investing

Experience is what you get, when you don't get what you want. Eighteen years ago, when I made my first angel investment, I wish I knew then what I know today. As a newly minted angel in 2000, I assumed that angel investing would be easy to jump into and become successful at. I was partially right… it was easy to jump into. Unfortunately, it took a little more work and learning to become successful.

I've had my share of luck and good outcomes, but I also learned many painful lessons along the way. Many of them would have been easy to avoid, had I understood a few key concepts. For this reason, Seraf Co-Founder Christopher Mirabile and I are determined to help new angels learn from our mistakes and the mistakes of others we have had the opportunity to observe from our perch at the center of a busy angel ecosystem. Angel 101 and Angel 201 are based on courses we developed over many years and regularly teach to the members of our angel network, Launchpad Venture Group. They are fun, interactive two hour sessions with lots of Q&A from the audience. They are rewarding classes to teach because Christopher and I feed off each other's energy, tell war stories, and try our best to keep the audience engaged and entertained. And we learn so much from our members' questions and observations. What a great way to learn!

## A Little History

Angel investing has been around forever, but it started to break into the mainstream in popular American culture in the early 2000s. It started with stories of individuals striking it rich from investments in companies like eBay, Yahoo, PayPal and Google. Silicon Valley garnered most of the headlines, but angel investors increased their activity in other technology centers such as Boston and Seattle and eventually San Diego, Austin and New York.

Then, the media began writing about celebrities and athletes making angel investments. Ashton Kutcher, Bono, Kanye West, Justin Timberlake and many others placed their celebrity endorsement on dozens of startups hoping to add to their fortunes. A few of these investments turned out well, but most ended up as write-offs.

Today, one of the most watched shows on TV is Shark Tank, which is based on a popular worldwide TV series called Dragons' Den. More than 8 million viewers tune into Shark Tank every week to watch a reality TV show where entrepreneurs present to a panel of investors, called Sharks. Leaving aside the obvious issues of deliberately and distastefully using entrepreneurs in need of money as a source of public entertainment, you have to wonder if things are getting a bit overheated when popular culture embraces an esoteric activity like investing in startup companies! Has angel investing jumped the proverbial shark?? (pun intended!)

All this press and publicity for angel investing makes it sound like anyone can walk onto the scene and be successful picking companies and throwing a few thousand dollars at the entrepreneur with expectations of riches to follow. Experienced angel investors know this gross misperception will lead to a lot of disappointment. Angel investing isn't easy. Sure, you might get lucky once or twice, but that's no different than betting on a roulette wheel. So for all of you who are thinking about becoming an angel investor and want to learn to do it right, or for those who are looking to brush up your skills, we have prepared two comprehensive courses to give you a solid foundation going forward.

## What's in this Book?

There are two main sections in this book. The first section includes the slides for an in-depth, 2 hour class that we call "**Angel 101**". This class will introduce you to six key topics that all angel investors need to understand as they make investments and ultimately build a successful portfolio of early stage companies:

1. What an angel is and where they invest
2. Financial concepts used to build a successful angel portfolio
3. The angel investing process from start to finish
4. Where to find interesting investment opportunities
5. Why it's important to undertake due diligence before investing
6. The importance of investing both financial and human capital

The second section includes the slides for an in-depth, 2 hour class that we call "**Angel 201**". In this course, we dig deep into helping you understand the basic concepts involved in negotiating a deal with an early stage company and how these companies are financed from inception to successful exit. The course will provide detailed material in six main areas:

1. Introduction to investment deal terms on a termsheet
2. Introduction to establishing a fair valuation for a startup company
3. Company capitalization tables
4. Thinking about later follow-on rounds
5. Ways in which companies exit and return capital to investors
6. Some key angel-focused tax issues

In addition to these two slide decks, we include an appendix with tools and guides that help investors improve their returns. In the appendix you will find:

1. Early Stage Investment Portfolio Modeling Tool
2. Due Diligence Report Template
3. Due Diligence Checklist
4. Customer Reference Check Questionnaire
5. Management Assessment Questionnaire

6. Guidelines for Successful Board Meetings
7. Deal Terms Expectations Summary Memo
8. A Guide to Angel Investing Docs: Preferred Stock Deal
9. A Guide to Angel Investing Docs: Convertible Debt Deal
10. Sample Termsheet: Preferred Stock
11. Sample Termsheet: Convertible Note
12. Capitalization Tables with Waterfall Analysis
13. Valuation Modeling Tool
14. Exit Planning Guide

By mastering the materials in this book, you should be confident in launching your angel career and building a profitable early stage company portfolio.

# INTRODUCTION TO ANGEL INVESTING

Angel 101

# Angel Capital Association
World's Largest Association of Active Accredited Investors

**ABOUT US**

*Vision*

ACA is recognized as the trusted authority in angel investing.

▶ 13,000+ Investors
▶ 250+ Organizations
▶ Every US State and 5 Canadian Provinces
▶ Individual Angels, Angel Groups, Accredited Platforms, Family Offices

---

**1 EVENTS**
Host many international, national and regional events a year

**2 EDUCATION**
Provide gold standard education for angels

**3 PUBLIC POLICY**
Leading voice for angels on public policy lobbying in Washington, DC

**4 DATA & RESEARCH**
Central resource for angel investing data and research

## Our Mission

Fuel the success of the accredited investor community through advocacy, education and connection building.

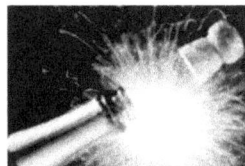

# Welcome Message

### Seraf's Philosophy

We believe investors in early stage companies should have access to best practices and professional tools to support the entrepreneurial community worldwide and achieve superior outcomes.

Insights and education, combined with powerful portfolio management tools allow investors to understand their investing better, learn faster and make necessary adjustments to select the highest quality opportunities and drive superior returns.

---

### About the Authors

Ham is Co-Founder of Seraf and the Chairman of Launchpad Venture Group, a Boston-based angel group. Through his involvement with Launchpad, Ham has built a personal portfolio of 50+ early stage investments. In addition, he is a board member or board observer with 5 early stage companies.

Christopher is Chair Emeritus of the Angel Capital Association and Managing Director of Launchpad Venture Group. He helps manage Launchpad's portfolio of 70+ companies, he has personally invested in over 65 start-up companies, and is a limited partner in four specialized angel funds. Christopher is a board member, advisor and mentor to numerous start-ups, and a frequent panelist and speaker on entrepreneurship and angel-related topics.

Seraf Co-Founders
Ham Lord & Christopher Mirabile

## Presentation Overview

**1  INTRODUCTION**
Angel 101: Basic concepts of angel investing

**2  GETTING STARTED**
What is an angel and where do they invest?

**3  PORTFOLIO THEORY**
Building a successful angel portfolio

**4  INVESTMENT PROCESS**
The steps from first meeting to investment

**5  DEAL FLOW**
Finding interesting companies

**6  DUE DILIGENCE**
Evaluating investment opportunities

**7  ANGEL ROLES**
Investing human capital

**8  APPENDIX**
Tools, templates & resources

---

## INTRODUCTION

This course gives prospective investors a complete overview of key elements of the fascinating and rewarding angel world:

- Time commitment
- Financial commitment
- Skills
- Risks

It's important to understand what you are getting into or your expectations might frustrate you

*"Luck is a matter of preparation meeting opportunity."* - Seneca

*"The more I practice, the luckier I get."* - Arnold Palmer

# Key Concepts in Angel 101

- What an angel is and where they invest
- Financial concepts used to build a successful angel portfolio
- The angel investing process from start to finish
- Where to find interesting investment opportunities
- Why it's important to undertake due diligence before investing
- The importance of investing both financial and human capital

# INTRODUCTION TO ANGEL INVESTING
## Getting Started

## How Does One Become an Angel?

Everyone has their own personal story of how they became an angel

Some common themes include:

- Helping a friend by investing time and money in her startup
- Networking or professional activities which lead to people with interests in helping entrepreneurs or impact investing
- Hearing from an acquaintance how much he/she enjoys angel investing and accepting an invitation to join his/her angel network

*For experienced, successful, energetic people who want to give back, many roads that lead to angel investing.*

## What Companies Do Angels Invest In?

Short answer… all types of companies are possible candidates.

However, there is large focus on high risk / high potential businesses

The businesses with the potential to deliver 10X+ returns to investors tend to have one or more of the following characteristics:

- Disruptive new technologies
- New fast-growing markets
- New disruptive business models

*To overcome inertia of "familiar & good enough," new products need to be an order of magnitude better faster or cheaper. It is hard to do that without tech.*

---

## At What Stage Do Angels Invest?

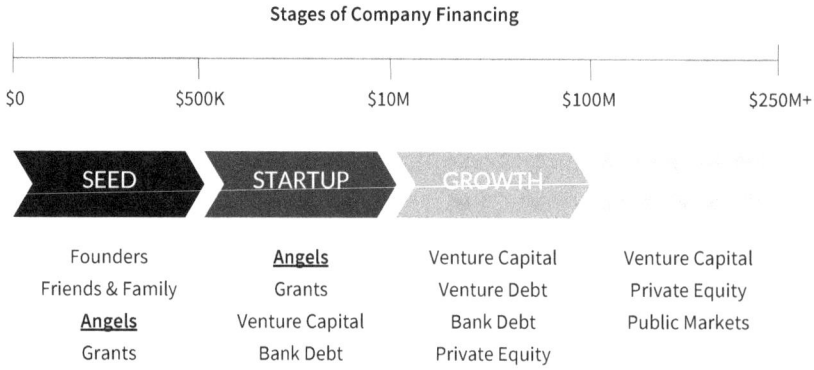

| Founders | Angels | Venture Capital | Venture Capital |
| Friends & Family | Grants | Venture Debt | Private Equity |
| Angels | Venture Capital | Bank Debt | Public Markets |
| Grants | Bank Debt | Private Equity | |

*Angels have finite financial capital combined with valuable human capital, so they tend to focus on the earliest stages where they can make a difference.*

# INTRODUCTION TO ANGEL INVESTING
## Portfolio Theory

---

## How Much Should I Invest?

Consider angel investing as part of your overall **asset allocation strategy**

- Public Company Stock, Real Estate, Collectables, Commodities
- Hedge Funds, Private Equity, Venture Capital

Illiquid private company investments (e.g. Angel Investments, VC) should represent a **minority percent** of your asset allocation

For the majority of angel investors who are not full time angel professionals, a 5% to 10% allocation to angel investments is sufficient and prudent

*Don't put more into angel investing than you can afford to lose.*

# How Many Investments Should I Make?

All successful portfolios are either diversified or *ridiculously lucky*.

**Diversification** is a core feature of all professional angel portfolios

- Expect to make a minimum of 10 investments
- But, diversification begins, not ends, at 10 companies - 20+ investments will greatly increase your likelihood of a positive overall return

*A single 10X return will pay for 9 mistakes.*

# Are There Other Diversification Factors?

Diversification is more than quantity. Consider building a portfolio with companies that are in different:

- Industries or sectors
- Stages of development
- Types of entrepreneurs
- Types of key risks

Invest in a few companies which allow you to be involved and leverage your expertise, and invest in some where you can afford to be more passive.

*Macro-economic cycles vary, as do industry cycles - a large and diverse portfolio will insulate you from business cycle swings.*

## How Do I Pace My Angel Investing?

Here is one example of the level of commitment it takes to build a portfolio of 10 to 20 companies:

- 3 to 5 new investments per year for initial 4 years
- Follow-on investments equalling $1 for every $1 invested in each company
- With $10K checks, you will invest between $30K and $100K per year
- Total amount invested will range between $200K and $400K

*To the brand new angel looking to put $75K into their first deal, I say "how about $10K into seven deals? You'll thank me later…"*

## How Do I Evaluate Risk vs. Return?

In every asset class, you are looking to understand overall risk vs. return

Angel investing is properly classified as high risk, with the potential of high returns.

Your goal is to recognize opportunities with the potential to deliver excess returns for the risks presented.

One hint: experienced angel investors tend to prefer **execution** type risks rather than more fundamental **technical or "science"** risks

*Will you be a low conviction angel with a "spray and pray" approach, or a high conviction angel with a more concentrated portfolio? Or somewhere between?*

## What's an Appropriate Return Given the Risks?

Angel investments are zero liquidity, long term, high risk investments.

Public blue chips may go down, but rarely go all the way to zero in a short span of time. Plus, they allow you to sell on the way down.

Therefore, angel returns must be higher than liquid investments like public stocks.

So, what should the return premium over public company stocks be?

- 5%, 10%, more?

*To understand likely returns, you need to analyze the capital structure, future capital requirements, and the exit potential for the company.*

## Source of Upside Potential? Early Rounds.

The basic edge of angels

- Time, patience, energy and skill
- Ability to get involved in very early rounds
- Invest in young companies with lower valuations

And then to follow those early investments with smart money: growth consumes cash; companies tend to raise more than once

- Seed rounds are the earliest independent money
- Mainstream angel rounds are typically $250K-$2.5M
- Later rounds may be Angel, VC or both

*If things are going well, later rounds are merely arithmetically dilutive; if things are going poorly, they are economically AND arithmetically dilutive.*

## Should I Invest in Earliest Early Seed Round?

Early seed rounds are hard to price and typically deliberately overvalue the company in order to make the "founder economics" work.

- Risk/Reward ratio is often *better* in the *later* rounds
- But, by making an initial investment, you gain the option to invest in future rounds
- With the hottest opportunities, if you did not invest in the seed round, you may not be able to get in at all.

*The price of admission in the hottest deals is often the small check you wrote in the early seed round.*

## Tracking Angel Investing Returns

Angel Investing returns are more challenging to track than public markets.

There have been multiple research efforts based on limited data

- Largest and most formal report (2007) by Wiltbank and Boeker using 3,097 investments from 538 angels... Shows a 27% annual rate of return

*More research and data is needed to better understand angel returns. The ACA Data Analytics Project is focused on this research.*

## Best Returns Correlated with Work, Process

Wiltbank / Boeker study indicates that angel returns are better when angels:

- Put in 20-40 hours of diligence
- Had expertise or access to expertise
- Interacted with portfolio companies with coaching, connections, etc.

*A risky, illiquid and labor-intensive asset class had better offer superior returns!*

---

## Distribution of Company Exits - Multiples

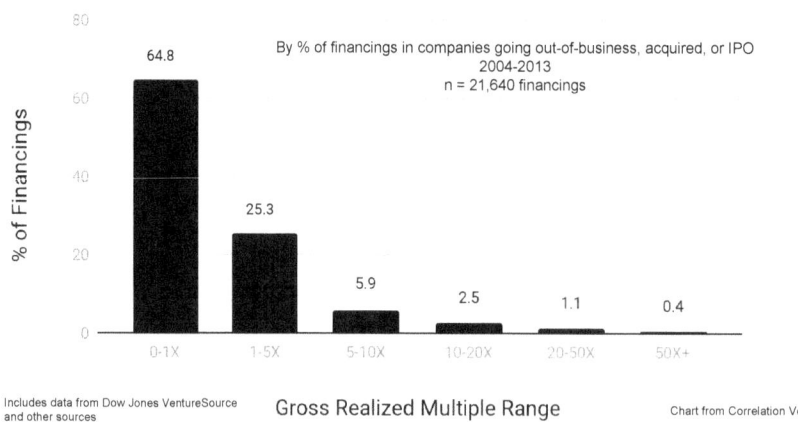

Right-Skewed Distribution of US Venture Returns

By % of financings in companies going out-of-business, acquired, or IPO
2004-2013
n = 21,640 financings

| Gross Realized Multiple Range | % of Financings |
|---|---|
| 0-1X | 64.8 |
| 1-5X | 25.3 |
| 5-10X | 5.9 |
| 10-20X | 2.5 |
| 20-50X | 1.1 |
| 50X+ | 0.4 |

Includes data from Dow Jones VentureSource and other sources. Chart from Correlation Ventures.

*Less than 1 out of 20 venture-backed companies turns into a home run.*

## Distribution of Company Exits - Dollars

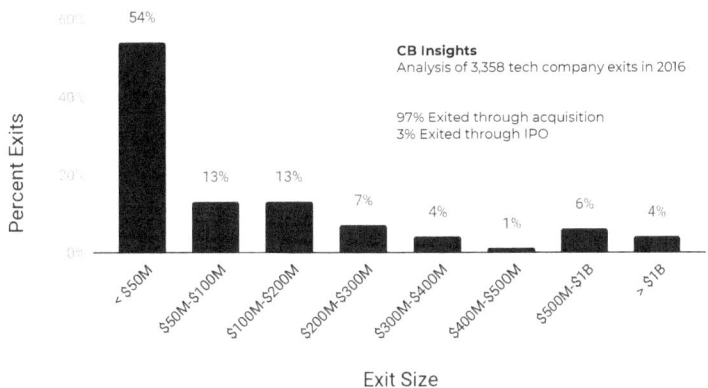

2016 Global Tech Exits

**CB Insights**
Analysis of 3,358 tech company exits in 2016

97% Exited through acquisition
3% Exited through IPO

*These exits include only VC exits. There are many more exits of angel backed companies in the sub $50M range.*

---

## Building a Successful Angel Portfolio

If you build a portfolio of 20 companies, what can you expect?

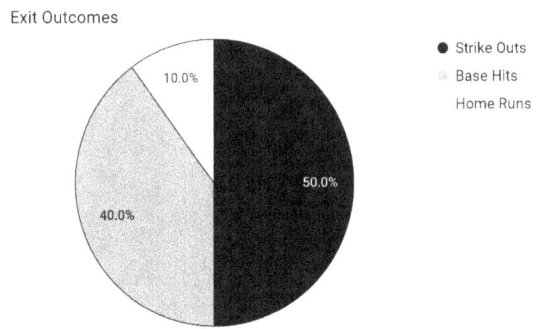

Exit Outcomes
- Strike Outs
- Base Hits
- Home Runs

*If you don't perform due diligence and add human capital to support your investments, you limit your likelihood of achieving these results.*

# Example: One Path to Top Quintile 3X Return

There are **many paths** to a 3X return

Here's one example where we invest the same amount ($10,000) in each of 10 companies:

- 5 companies fail and return $10,000 in total
- 3 companies are small exits and return $90,000  (~$30,000 each)
- 1 company is a medium exit and returns $50,000
- 1 company is a home run and returns $150,000

If you add up the returns, it equals $300,000 for your $100,000 invested. Your IRR will depend on how fast it all happens.

*Without one 10X+ home run in your portfolio, it's extremely difficult to achieve a 3X return.*

# INTRODUCTION TO ANGEL INVESTING
## Investment Process

---

## Elements of an Angel Investment Process

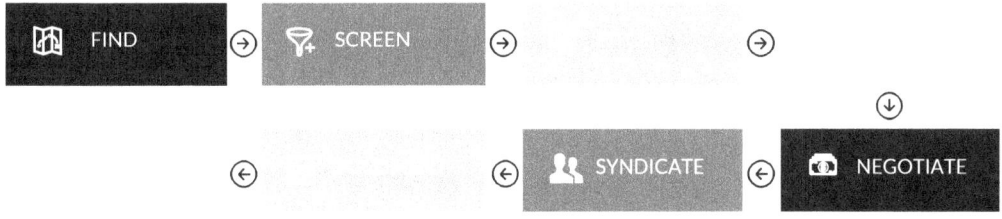

*Most startups fail, and they take a lot of investment dollars with them. It takes a solid process to build good deals with a superior chance of return.*

## 1) Finding Great Companies

Getting access to great companies requires building a network of:

- Entrepreneurs who recommend you to their peers
- Investors looking for syndication partners
- Other angels in your group, fund or network active in the community
- Service providers such as lawyers and accountants

*Reputation and referrals are the linchpins of superior deal flow for angels.*

## 2) Screening

Screening is the process of filtering potential wheat from the chaff

It's a process to help focus your time on companies which:

- Fit with your investment focus areas
- Have true upside potential
- No obvious red flags or show-stoppers
- Relatively attractive compared to other companies in your funnel

*There are more interesting companies than you can spend time on. Your goal should be to spend less time on more deals, and more time on fewer deals.*

## 3) Pitching

Pitching evolved because it is a very efficient way to reach a wide variety of angel investor types

- Audience ranges from a few solo investors up to a large angel group
- Entrepreneur delivers a 10-15 minute presentation followed by Q&A
- Main purpose of the pitch is to "set the hook" so investors will move to the next step in the process

*A best practice for all investors is to be decisive and transparent with a go/no-go decision shortly after the pitch.*

## 4) Due Diligence

Some angels might invest after just a pitch, but…

Most investors will undertake some level of due diligence,

Main purpose of diligence is to spot the easily avoidable mistakes and

Document and check the key assumptions you are making.

*Human nature is quick to grasp how things could go well, but slower to appreciate the more subtle ways in which things could go wrong.*

## 5) Negotiating

Some level of negotiation typically begins before diligence is complete

Key deal terms are discussed to make sure both sides are in same ballpark

- **Deal Structure** - preferred stock vs. convertible note
- **Valuation** - what is the company worth today?
- **Governance** - what will the board look like?

Once completed, negotiations should result in a mutually acceptable termsheet which can be shared with the final diligence report

*Negotiation is mostly entrepreneur education about key risks followed by agreement about how to allocate them.*

## 6) Deal Syndication

The lead investor will work with the entrepreneur to:

- Get a sense for how much investor interest is currently engaged
- How much additional money needs to be found
- Find other investors needed to fill up the remainder of the round

*A great deal lead puts together a market acceptable set of terms that allows a group of like-minded investors to come into alignment around a deal.*

## 7) Deal Documents

Before checks are written:

- Definitive legal documents are prepared based on "instructions" embodied in the termsheet
- Typically a 2 to 4 week timeline for drafting and negotiating legal docs

*The termsheet giveth but the deal documents taketh away (or at least narrow)... Deal documents are the definitive contracts you agree to - read them. Get help if you have questions, but don't rely on the termsheet.*

## 8) Closing

The company and the lead investor set a closing date and process

Key elements to this step include a set of clearly written closing instructions related to signing documents and sending funds

*Creating a good closing package is somewhat of an art. Done well it can be orderly and efficient. Done poorly it can lead to frustrations, mistakes, and deal delays.*

# The Critical Final Stage - Post Investment

But wait… you are not done just yet!

Once you are an investor, you have every incentive to help in any way you can

- Mentoring
- Introductions
- Board service

*Unlike with public companies, data and experience teaches that helping your angel companies can have a significant effect on your returns.*

# INTRODUCTION TO ANGEL INVESTING
## Deal Flow

---

## How Do You Find a Fishing Guide?

Wherever you live, there should be a nucleus of an entrepreneurial community

Networking to find experienced angels will help forge early connections

National organizations (e.g. ACA, NACO, HBAN, EBAN) are key resources

*To catch a fish you need to know where to look. Great guides can take you to the best fishing holes.*

## Where Are the Best Fishing Holes?

Best spots are most commonly found in locations with strong entrepreneurial communities

- Universities with business schools or robust entrepreneurship programs
- Incubators and Accelerators
- Regional Meetups
- Co-Working Spaces

*Entrepreneurship communities are like hives that feed and support themselves. Find the centers of activity so you can find the fastest moving opportunities.*

## Do You Know What You Are Fishing For?

This is a critical question that all angels need to ask and answer

Active angels should develop two key checklists

- **Will Invest**: What you look for in a company and a deal
- **Won't Invest**: What are the "showstoppers" where you say "no"

*There is nothing entrepreneurs despise more than a tire-kicking angel who takes up a ton of their time but never invests.*

## Angel Funds

Angel Funds are another approach to angel investing.

- Managers oversee the fund and report out to investors
- Typically less of a time commitment for the individual angel
- Can supplement direct investment to build a more diversification
- Funds do have fees & carry that impact returns to investors

*Like networks, well-run funds can leverage the efficiencies of working together.*

## Equity Crowdfunding - Accredited Platforms

Can be a good fit for angels who:

- Have limited access to good deal flow, or
- Are looking for non-local or specialty deals

Challenges and Issues:

- Not easy to meet founders during due diligence
- Difficult to add your human capital post-investment
- Platforms vary in fees charged, structure, amount of support given

*Platforms can turn up interesting deals, but caveat emptor.*

## Equity Crowdfunding - Non Accredited

Companies can publicly solicit investment from non-accredited investors

Strict limits on annual amounts investor may invest

Strict annual amounts company may raise

Strict disclosure requirements for companies

Transactions must happen on special brokerage platforms

*Non-accredited crowdfunding is a new phenomenon with very uncertain risk/return profile.*

## Equity Crowdfunding - Non-Accredited

Expensive money compared to accredited investor angel deals

Risk of adverse selection - last resort for some companies?

Reg CF is a useful framework for situations where:
- Group of **stakeholders** wish to create a joint enterprise
- Transaction costs are less important than the underlying cause (deal is more about a quasi-public-good)

*Unaccredited crowdfunding may prove to be more about **stake**holders than **stock**holders.*

# INTRODUCTION TO ANGEL INVESTING
## Due Diligence

---

## Why Do We Do It?

A well executed diligence effort increases angel investment returns

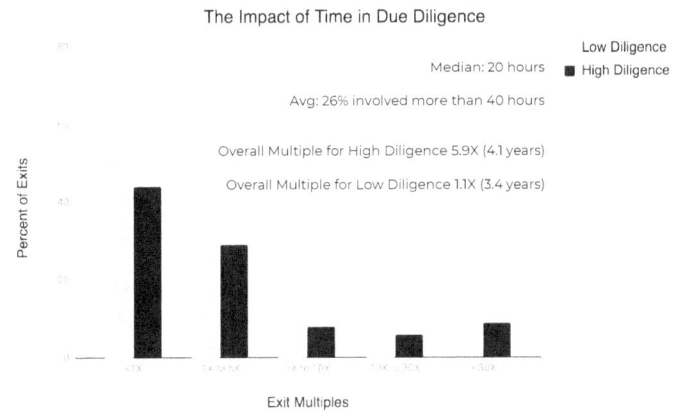

The Impact of Time in Due Diligence

Median: 20 hours
Avg: 26% involved more than 40 hours

Overall Multiple for High Diligence 5.9X (4.1 years)
Overall Multiple for Low Diligence 1.1X (3.4 years)

*Mistakes are unavoidable, but racking up easily avoidable mistakes will hurt your overall returns.*

## Why Due Diligence is Important

Diligence is not about removing all risk and eliminating all mistakes

Investing at an early stage - lots of unknowns, there will be failures

Diligence is about spotting and avoiding the ***obvious*** mistakes

*It's easy to imagine why things might work. It takes effort to grasp subtle and complex ways things can go wrong.*

## During Due Diligence, You Will…

Spend time with the management team

Educate yourself on the market

Understand the psyche of the target customer

Ask common sense questions

*There is no right amount of diligence. Any diligence you do is better than none at all.*

## 3 Guiding Principles of Due Diligence

Identify Key Risks

Develop the Investment Thesis

Acknowledge "What Needs to Be Believed" to Invest

*Forcing yourself to acknowledge what needs to be believed provides a very powerful reality check.*

## Main Areas of Focus in Due Diligence

**Team**: Are they an "A" team or a "B" team?

**Product**: Are they selling a "Need to Have" or a "Nice to Have"?

**Market**: Is the market big enough to support a decent exit?

*No plan survives contact with the enemy. A great team can assess, learn and adapt quickly to survive and thrive. A good CEO pivots… a great CEO pivots in a capital efficient way.*

# 10 Key Risks in Early Stage Investing

Risk is an inherent part, and necessary ingredient in all successful companies

The question is whether you understand the risks the company is taking, and have strategies to mitigate them

*Without risk there can be no reward.*

# Team Risk

Conduct a thorough leadership assessment

- Review resumes
- Perform provided and "blind" reference checks
- Spend one-on-one time with the CEO

Look for people with integrity, tenacity, book learning and street smarts

*I'd rather invest in an A team with a B plan, than a B team with an A plan.*

## Technical Risk

Does the widget exist yet? If not, is there a chance that it may be impossible to build?

Customer benefits matter. Benefits should approach a 10x improvement for the typical user.

*A company that can hold their own in a detailed product roadmap review has a lot less technical risk than one that can't.*

## Market Adoption Risk

Ask customers and prospects the following...

- What problem does this product solve for you?
- Where does solving this problem fall on your priority list?
- Is your company generally an early adopter or late adopter?

Look for genuine demand or "pull" from a large enough segment of customers

*If you build it, will they come?*

## Future Financing Risk

Know the macro market for financing

Know the benchmarks applied by those providing future capital

Look beyond the current round of financing, and ask the following:

- How much additional financing will the company need?
- Where will that money come from?
- Will it be available on reasonable terms?
- Who are the right investors for the company going forward?

*Build a reasonable plan with the current financing round that allows some room for error.*

## Regulatory Risk

Are there any necessary permissions (e.g. FDA approval) to operate this business?

Not all regulatory situations introduce risk - sometimes they provide tailwinds; new rules may hasten adoption of a company's solution.

*Regulatory approvals take time and money. Understand what is involved and watch for possible changes in the regulatory environment.*

## Competitive Risk

Understand the company's relative attractiveness alongside their competitors, and carve out a space with some enduring value

Competitors help educate the market, but they also

- Drive up the length of the sales cycle
- Undermine pricing power and compress margins
- Drive additional spend on R&D

*Show me an entrepreneur with no competition and I will show you an entrepreneur with no market.*

## Intellectual Property Risk

A lack of awareness and sophistication about IP can be an important risk factor in diligence

**Defensive analysis**: Are they free to operate without infringing on someone's IP?

**Offensive analysis**: Can they build IP to protect their space and block competitors?

*Can the company develop patents as counter-claims or trading cards in case of an attack on the company?*

## Legal Risk

What legal issues might be critical for this early stage company?
- Capitalization & Ownership
- Intellectual Property
- Regulatory Compliance
- Third Party Contracts
- Employment Matters

*Does the company have its house in order? Is there enough attention being paid to important details?*

## Alignment Risk

How do you make sure the goals of investors and company founders are in alignment on the following key issues?
- Long term objectives
- Use of funds
- Long term financing path
- Exit assumptions and strategy

*Is everyone singing from the same page of the hymnal?*

## Exit Risk

Exit Strategies
- What are the exit opportunities for the company?
- Who will buy this company?
- When will they buy them?
- What will they value them for?

*Equity investment is a loan the ultimate buyer of the company is expected to pay back.*

## Develop the Investment Thesis

**Potential** - How big is the potential theoretical opportunity?

**Probability** - How likely is the company to achieve breakthrough success?

**Period** - How long are you going to have to wait?

*All things being equal, we want companies most likely to be the biggest in the shortest amount of time.*

## Acknowledge "What Needs to Be Believed"

Core of this exercise is a test… we must ask ourselves:

- Have we identified the key risks?
- Do we understand the premise of the deal (i.e. the investment thesis)?

*Are we fooling ourselves, or is there some kind of balanced logic to this deal?*

## Learning the Hard Way

A handful of avoidable due diligence mistakes

- **Team**: Confusing likability or prior accomplishments with the competence needed to pull off the current task
- **Market**: Confusing early adopter excitement with true market pull
- **Timing**: Is this the right time for this idea?
- **Product**: Incomplete understanding of the dynamics in the target market

*Experience is what you get when you don't get what you want.*

# INTRODUCTION TO ANGEL INVESTING
## Angel Roles

---

## Angel Roles

Majority of entrepreneurs only look to angels for financial capital

But, smart investors are an excellent source of human capital

- Corporate Board Member
- Mentor
- Advisory Board

*If none of the investors in a startup have the ability to add valuable human capital, you probably shouldn't invest.*

## How Does a Board Member Add Value?

Board directors can help their portfolio companies be successful by:

- Recruiting senior management
- Fund raising
- Strategic advice
- Making connections and getting initial customers
- Evaluating the CEO
- Managing risk
- Ensuring a successful exit

*It is impossible to overstate the value of having some "been there, done that" people around to provide tips, perspective and advice.*

## What's the Time Commitment?

A board seat is the most significant time commitment for an angel

During a typical year, you will spend 100+ hours with the following:

- 6 to 12 board meetings per year
- Weekly or bi-weekly phone calls with the CEO
- Unscheduled events: candidate interviews, fundraising, etc.

*Being on a startup board is a huge commitment. If someone tells you they are on more than 3-5 boards at once, they are almost certainly not doing it right.*

## What is a Mentor?

The universe of mentors can be divided into three categories

- **Industry Expert**: Deep understanding of industry, market or technology and can give strategic advice and make crucial introductions
- **Company Builder**: Successful track record in building and scaling startup companies
- **Personal Growth**: Help CEO with professional development

*There is no need to choose - every founder should have at least one of each kind of mentor.*

## Matching Mentors with Entrepreneurs

A mentor is the equivalent of a wingman… someone who has your back

You know there is a good match when:

- Entrepreneur feels empathy even when receiving critical input
- Mentor makes time and is responsive to inquiries
- Mentor is truly engaged and helpful to the entrepreneur

*Before formalizing a relationship, make sure you do a little due diligence on your entrepreneur.*

## Key Sins of Angel Investors

The list is VERY long, but here are two biggies:

- Be careful about wasting the time of an entrepreneur
- Just because you are more experienced doesn't mean you should take advantage of a rookie entrepreneur

*Respect, and a service-oriented, pay-it-forward attitude are the keys to building a good reputation as an investor.*

# INTRODUCTION TO ANGEL INVESTING
## Appendix

---

## Resources - Modeling Tool for Early Stage Investment Portfolios

A successful early stage investment portfolio has a mix of strikeouts, base hits and home runs. So how is it possible for an early stage investor to build a successful portfolio compiled from companies that produce such widely different financial returns? To answer that question, we pulled together a simple modeling tool that helps you visualize how the probable returns play out and interact to produce an overall portfolio return.

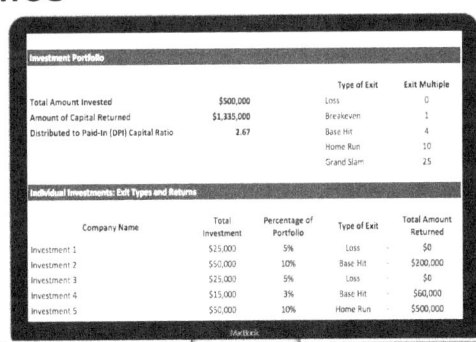

**Download**
Modeling Tool
bit.ly/Seraf_Portfolio_Modeling_Tool

# Resources - Due Diligence Checklist

Designed as a quick reference guide to help steer you through the various aspects of diligence. This due diligence checklist covers key items such as:

- Information and documents you need to request from the company
- Tasks your due diligence team needs to perform
- Questions you need to ask of management, customers, references and partners

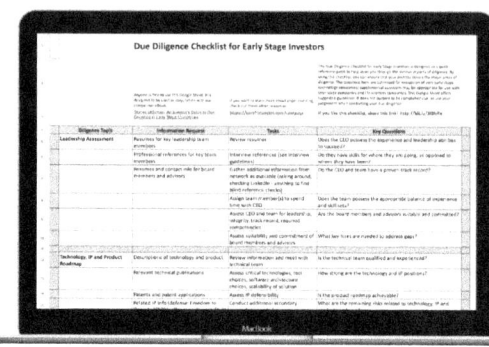

**Download Checklist**
bit.ly/Due_Diligence_Checklist

# Resources - Due Diligence Report Template

The due diligence report template is focused on 11 major topics that should be researched and understood when performing due diligence on an early stage technology company.

For each topic, we provide you with an explanation of the topic as well as example questions that may make sense to discuss in the remarks column.

**Download Report Template**
bit.ly/DueDiligenceReportTemplate

# Resources - Management Team Assessment

Questionnaire designed to help guide you through your team reference checks

Focus on questions related to the CEO's:

- Strengths and Weaknesses
- Communications Skills
- Coachability
- Stability
- Domain Expertise
- Complementary Skills on Management Team

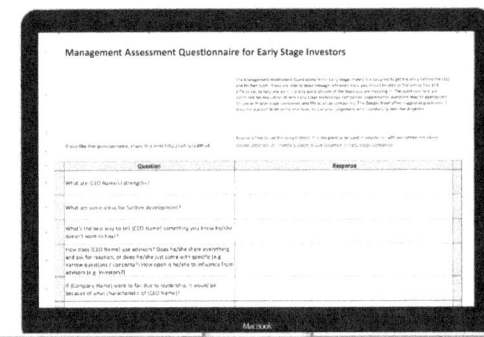

**Download Questionnaire**
bit.ly/ManagementQuestionnaire

---

# Resources - Customer Reference Checks

Questionnaire designed to help guide you through product-related questions

Focus is on questions related to solving a customer's key problems:

- Problem Being Solved and Priority for Solving
- Purchase Reasons and Goals
- Expected ROI and Value to the Customer
- Competitive Factors
- Impressions of the Company and Its Product

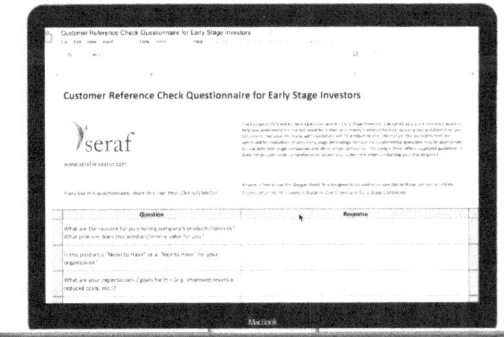

**Download Questionnaire**
bit.ly/CustomerReferenceChecks

# Resources - Guidelines for Successful Board Meetings

Running a successful board meeting requires planning and discipline. Which in turn requires some experience and some guidelines. Without this preparation, you will waste precious time focusing on the wrong things. To help you orchestrate great board meetings, we pulled together a collection of well-tested guidelines that will make any early stage company board more productive.

Download Guidelines
bit.ly/BoardMeetingGuidelines

## The Seraf Compass

# Continue Your Angel Education and Improve Your Investing Skills

The Seraf Compass guides early stage investors in making better investing decisions, minimizing risk and improving returns

**Introduction to Angel Investing Articles**
bit.ly/Angel101Articles

**Introduction to Angel Investing eBook**
bit.ly/Angel101eBook

**Introduction to Angel Investing Hardcopy Book**
bit.ly/HardCopyBooks

**Introduction to Angel Investing Tools**
bit.ly/SerafToolbox

---

## The Seraf Compass

From Investment to Exit: Insights, news, thought leadership and in-depth resources for early stage investors

**ACCESS OUR CONTENT**
- BLOG
- BOOKS and eBOOKS
- TOOLS

FOLLOW US ON SOCIAL MEDIA

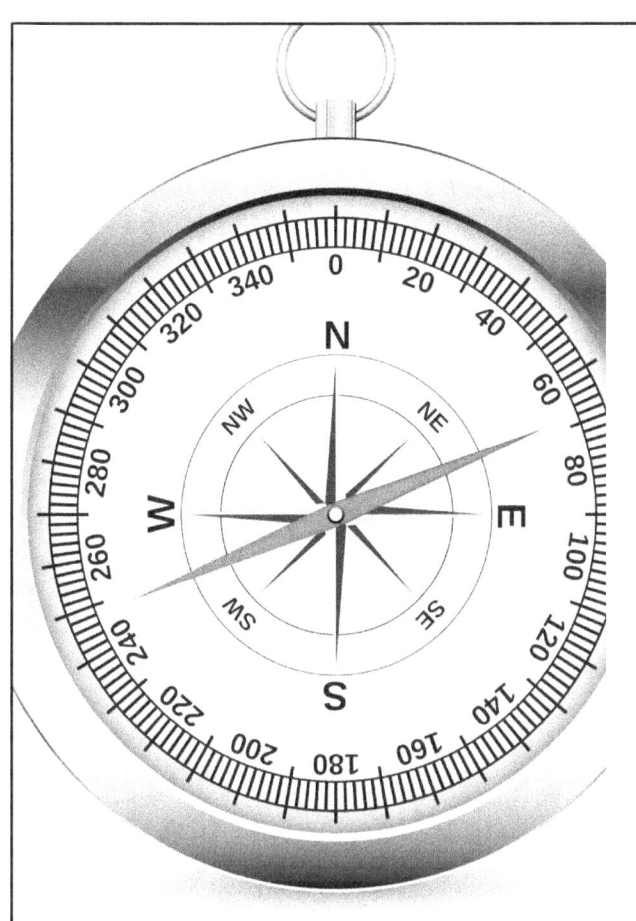

# Books from Seraf

### Fundamentals of Angel Investing
A Guide to the Principles, Skills and Concepts Every Angel Investor Needs to Succeed

### Angel Investing by the Numbers
Valuation, Capitalization, Portfolio Construction and Startup Economics

### Leaders Wanted: Making Startup Deals Happen
Advanced Techniques in Deal Leadership and Due Diligence for Early Stage Investors

### Guide, Advise and Inspire: How Startup Boards Drive Growth and Exits
An Overview of the Principles, Skills and Concepts Every Early Stage Company Board Member Needs to Succeed

### Venture Capital: A Practical Guide
A Guide to Fund Formation and Management

## PORTFOLIO MANAGEMENT FOR EARLY STAGE INVESTORS

All Your Info. One Place. Smart Investing.

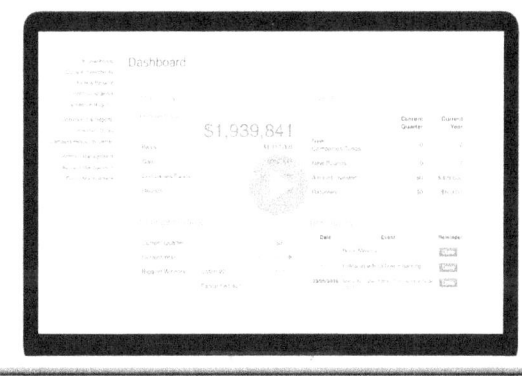

## WHAT MAKES SERAF DIFFERENT

**Easy Workflow**
Seraf guides you through a few easy steps to get your portfolio up and running quickly. Get an overview, develop insights and generate reports in no time.

**Deep Experience**
Designed by active, early stage investors with over 25 years experience in fund creation and management, the Seraf team understands the complexities of today's early stage investment landscape.

**Narrowly Focused Solution**
Developed specifically to meet the needs of early stage investors, Seraf provides the tools YOU need to manage your portfolio efficiently.

51

## AUTHORS

Hambleton Lord

Christopher Mirabile

## CONTACT US

www.seraf-investor.com

www.angelcapitalassociation.org

# INTRODUCTION TO ANGEL INVESTING

Angel 201

# Angel Capital Association
## World's Largest Association of Active Accredited Investors

**ABOUT US**

*Vision*

ACA is recognized as the trusted authority in angel investing.

- 13,000+ Investors
- 250+ Organizations
- Every US State and 5 Canadian Provinces
- Individual Angels, Angel Groups, Accredited Platforms, Family Offices

---

**1 EVENTS**
Host many international, national and regional events a year

**2 EDUCATION**
Provide gold standard education for angels

**3 PUBLIC POLICY**
Leading voice for angels on public policy lobbying in Washington, DC

**4 DATA & RESEARCH**
Central resource for angel investing data and research

**Our Mission**

Fuel the success of the accredited investor community through advocacy, education and connection building.

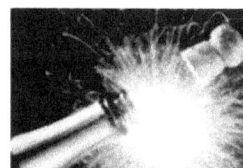

# Welcome Message

### Seraf's Philosophy

We believe investors in early stage companies should have access to best practices and professional tools to support the entrepreneurial community worldwide and achieve superior outcomes.

Insights and education, combined with powerful portfolio management tools allow investors to understand their investing better, learn faster and make necessary adjustments to select the highest quality opportunities and drive superior returns.

---

### About the Authors

Ham is Co-Founder of Seraf and the Chairman of Launchpad Venture Group, a Boston-based angel group. Through his involvement with Launchpad, Ham has built a personal portfolio of 50+ early stage investments. In addition, he is a board member or board observer with 5 early stage companies.

Christopher is Chair Emeritus of the Angel Capital Association and Managing Director of Launchpad Venture Group. He helps manage Launchpad's portfolio of 70+ companies, he has personally invested in over 65 start-up companies, and is a limited partner in four specialized angel funds. Christopher is a board member, advisor and mentor to numerous start-ups, and a frequent panelist and speaker on entrepreneurship and angel-related topics.

Seraf Co-Founders
Ham Lord & Christopher Mirabile

## Presentation Overview

**1 INTRODUCTION**
What you can expect from this course

**2 TERMSHEETS**
A simple framework for a complex subject

**3 CAPITALIZATION TABLES**
Who owns what

**4 VALUATIONS**
Approach to valuing an early stage company

**5 FOLLOW-ON THEORY**
Knowing when to double down

**6 EXITS**
Start ups are bought not sold

**7 ANGELS AND TAXES**
Key concepts for minimizing taxes

**8 APPENDIX**
Tools, templates & resources

---

## Introduction

This course is targeted at angels who already understand these basics from Angel 101:

- Getting started and finding deal flow
- Due diligence and the investment process
- Portfolio construction
- Angel roles and the importance of human capital

## Key Concepts in Angel 201

In this class we introduce more advanced concepts around:

- Understanding deal terms on a termsheet
- Establishing a fair valuation for a startup company
- Company capitalization tables
- Thinking about later follow-on rounds
- Company exits
- Some key angel-focused tax issues

# INTRODUCTION TO ANGEL INVESTING
## Termsheets

## Types of Entities Angels Invest In

Angels can invest in different corporate entities

Two most common categories of entity are:

- Traditional C Corporation
- Limited Liability Company (LLC)

Pass through S Corps can be used, but generally only temporarily

Sole proprietorships and Partnerships (including LLPs) not appropriate

*Keep it simple. C Corps are the norm for good reasons.*

## Types of Securities Angels Invest In

Angels typically invest using one of three different deal structures:

- Investors **purchase stock** in a company (e.g. Preferred or Common Stock)
- Investors **lend money** to a company that is expected to convert into stock at a future time (e.g Convertible Note - discussed at length below)
- Investors **purchase a derivative security** that is intended to convert into stock at later date (e.g a SAFE, KISS or a warrant)

- Note: in recent years, it has also been possible for investors to **purchase tokens** through an Initial Coin Offering (ICO) - whole other subject

*It is usually not a question of whether you will end up with an ownership percentage, but rather how directly you will get there.*

## What It Means to Own Stock

Stock deals offer near perfect alignment between investors and founders

Investors don't win unless founders win, and vise versa

Implications:

- Exit orientation rather than dividend orientation
- Extensively customizable
- Some complexity requiring some experience and mastery

*Stock ownership is a marriage: for better or worse, in sickness and in health.*

## What is a Termsheet?

Long used by VCs, termsheets are used in most angel financings

The company and investors write down **key terms** in a document to:
- Facilitate negotiation of key issues
- Used to outline and document agreed key deal points
- Serve as basis for soliciting investor interest
- Act as a guide for use by counsel drafting definitive legal docs (termsheets themselves are not binding unless stated)

*The termsheet is the short but dense and jargony recipe the lawyers will follow when they create the definitive deal documents.*

## What is a Termsheet?

Termsheets are typically drafted by a "lead investor" who has expertise

Can either be done collaboratively or delivered unilaterally then negotiated

Important to get it right and appropriate for the market

Investor etiquette is to respect someone else's termsheet - otherwise chaos

*Get help if you are unsure - termsheets can set irreversible things in motion that cannot be walked back from.*

# It's Easier with a Framework

Termsheets cover a ton of topics, but…

ALL termsheet issues can be put into one of four buckets:

**Management & Control**

**Investor Rights & Protection**

**Deal Economics**

**Exits & Liquidity**

---

# Investor's Perspective & Concerns

**Management & Control**

Know what's going on in the company, have a say in decisions, and control founder behavior to avoid damaging the company.

**Investor Rights & Protection**

Make sure nobody diminishes the value of their investment or gets liquidity ahead of them.

**Deal Economics**

Make sure they get a big enough slice of the pie, get paid back first, put a time clock on the founders, and make sure employee options don't dilute them.

**Exits & Liquidity**

Make sure they get their money back in all possible scenarios, even if they have to force it.

# Founder's Perspective & Concerns

**Management & Control**

Make sure they don't lose control of the company and have a good fit/relationship with the investors.

**Investor Rights & Protection**

Don't want to risk losing ownership if they are fired or resign.

**Deal Economics**

Don't want to give away too much of the company or run out of money.

**Exits & Liquidity**

Don't want to have guarantees that put personal assets at risk.

---

# Overview of Key Terms to Address Investors' Concerns

**Management & Control**

- Board seats & control
- Information rights
- Founder vesting
- Founder non-competes

**Investor Rights & Protection**

- Anti-dilution
- Approval rights
- Participation rights
- ROFR & co-sale rights

**Deal Economics**

- Size of round
- Pre-money valuation
- Liquidation preference
- Dividends
- Option pool

**Exits & Liquidity**

- Rights to block founder transfers
- Drag-along rights
- Redemption rights
- Registration rights

# INTRODUCTION TO ANGEL INVESTING
## Capitalization Tables

---

## What is a Capitalization Table?

Comprehensive document that includes a record for all stakeholders

Tracks both equity ownership and outstanding debt

- Common and preferred stock
- Stock options and warrants
- Convertible debt

*The cap table is one of the most critical documents maintained by a company. It's vital for angels to understand it.*

## An Example Capitalization Table

| Name | Common Stock | Stock Options | Series A Preferred | Total Shares | Percent Outstanding | Percent Fully Diluted |
|---|---|---|---|---|---|---|
| Founder One | 1,500,000 | | 250,000 | 1,750,000 | 47.0% | 43.7% |
| Founder Two | 1,100,000 | | | 1,100,000 | 29.6% | 27.5% |
| Employee One | | 80,000 | | 80,000 | 2.2% | 2.0% |
| Employee Two | | 40,000 | | 40,000 | 1.1% | 1.0% |
| Investor One | | | 500,000 | 500,000 | 13.4% | 12.5% |
| Investor Two | | | 250,000 | 250,000 | 6.7% | 6.3% |
| Remaining Option Pool | | 280,000 | | 280,000 | | 7.0% |
| Total | 2,600,000 | 400,000 | 1,000,000 | 4,000,000 | 100% | 100% |
| Percent Ownership | 65% | 10% | 25% | 100% | | |

## Key Cap Table Terms - Valuations

**Pre-Money Valuation** - Valuation placed on company prior to an investment made in company

**Post-Money Valuation** - Effective valuation of company after an investment is made in company

**Price per Share** - Calculation based on taking post-money valuation and dividing it by the number of fully diluted shares

*Cap Table Arithmetic:*
Post-money = Pre-Money + Money Raised
Price per Share = Post-Money/Total Shares
Percent Owned = Money Raised/Post-Money

## Key Cap Table Terms - Security Types

**Common Stock** - Most basic form of equity ownership in a company is called common stock

**Preferred Stock** - A class or series of stock with special rights and privileges. Preferred stock is paid before common (but after debt) during a sale

**Convertible Preferred Stock** - Preferred stock which has option to either accept repayment preference OR convert to common stock (and be paid at the same time and rate as common) under a specified set of circumstances

---

## Key Cap Table Terms - Security Types

**Non-participating Preferred** - Preferred stock which has the right to be paid a multiple of original purchase price **OR** convert to common stock and "participate" in distribution to common

**Participating Preferred** - Preferred stock which has right to be paid original price (or more) **AND THEN** convert to common stock and "participate" in distribution to common as if it had simply converted in the first place

## Key Cap Table Terms - Security Types

**Stock Options** - Contractual right to purchase specified number of shares for a specified price at a specified future date or dates

**Warrants** - Nearly the same as options, but unlike options, warrants are typically one-offs and not issued under the terms of the stock option plan

**Restricted Stock** - Restricted stock has ownership restrictions which lapse over time. They are similar to stock options but have tax efficiency features

---

## Key Cap Table Terms - Share Counts

**Authorized Shares** - Number of shares duly authorized by company's board for present or future issuance

**Outstanding Shares** - Total number of shares issued -- only includes options and warrants that have been exercised

**Fully Diluted Shares** - Includes all granted options, restricted stock, warrants and often remainder of the option pool

## How Does a Cap Table Change Over Time?

As company routinely adds employees, directors and advisors, it will:

- Establish an option pool or increase size of current pool
- Option pool should represent 5% to 25% of fully diluted shares
- Grant options and restricted stock from the option pool

*Total shares outstanding is never static - options and restricted stock are constantly granted, vested, exercised. If precision is required, get an up-to-date cap table.*

## How Does a Cap Table Change Over Time?

As company raises both equity and debt, it will:

- Sell new shares or derivatives of an existing security (e.g. common shares or options, warrants or restricted common)
- Sell new shares of a new security (e.g. preferred shares)
- Issue convertible debt
- Issue warrants as part of either a debt or equity round

*Debt that doesn't convert to equity is not an official part of the equity capitalization, but it should be tracked in the Cap Table to understand how payments will be made to shareholders upon sale of the company.*

## Do Convertible Notes Affect the Cap Table?

Convertible notes are a type of debt that is meant to be paid back via conversion into shares of the company

Terms of conversion to shares can be complicated, so make sure you know how much convertible debt is outstanding and what terms apply to it.

*In almost all liquidation situations, debt holders are paid first before proceeds are paid to equity holders.*

## Effect of Liquidation Preference on Cap Table

Right to be paid "in preference to" (i.e. before) all other junior classes of stock

Can specify your preference as 1X your money, or a higher number such as 1.5X or 2X

*Multiple liquidation preferences (i.e. higher than 1X) can mean death for early investors. You might **think** you want them on your $1M round until someone later comes along wanting them on their $10M round.*

## Effect of Anti-Dilution Provision on Cap Table

Automatic retroactive adjustment of stock purchase price if there is a future down round

Typically effectuated by issuing additional stock to original buyers

Alternative approaches to calculating how much remedy to apply:
- Broad-based weighted average
- Narrow-based weighted average
- Full-ratchet

*Anti-dilution protection is cold comfort: if you need it, things are probably not going well for the company, plus the founder economics may be destroyed.*

---

## Effect of Dividend on Cap Table

Dividends may specify that they are paid in stock or cash

Dividends may specify they are paid in preference to common

Can be authorized but not paid except in certain trigger conditions

May specify a set rate; May or may not be cumulative

*A dividend accumulating in the background can make an enormous difference in the ultimate returns of different classes of stock.*

## What is a Waterfall Analysis?

Technical term used to describe process of calculating exact amounts each equity and debt holder will be paid upon company exit

- A series of sequential calculations
- Factors in various deal terms for all types of equity and debt

*Last money in is usually first money out, so you have to run the waterfall to figure out how much will be left for early rounds and common.*

# INTRODUCTION TO ANGEL INVESTING
## Valuations

---

## Why Valuation Matters

Some investors assert:

- If the company fails, valuation doesn't matter
- If the company hits it big, valuation doesn't matter
- Therefore, valuation doesn't matter

*This "binary view" is wrong. Valuation matters tremendously for three important reasons...*

## 1. Real World Results are not Binary

Vast majority of positive outcomes are in the middle - average M&A transaction is in $20-40M range

In these kinds of deals, early valuations are critical to returns

If you overpay going in (or over capitalize the company), you turn a nice win into a very mediocre result

*People overweight the potential for a huge outcome... Don't be one of those people.*

## 2. Dilution Kills You Even On the Winners

Even if you hit on a big one, later investors will supply far more of the capital than you will

Your ability to fund your pro-rata will taper off

The bigger a position you start with, the more of a position you will be able to hold onto despite dilution over time

*If the company really starts to take off, you will be helpless as you watch big money pour in and dilute your initial stake.*

## 3. High Post-Money Increases Failure Risk

Companies need a post-money valuation they can grow into

If the post-money gets ahead of reality, future money might not be available or only available on punitive terms

Avoid getting washed out by keeping the post-money reasonable and appropriate for stage and level of progress

*Better to under-promise and over-deliver than the other way around.*

## Startups are Different

Valuing mature companies is a science

- Discounted cash flow analysis
- Revenue or EBITDA multiples
- Asset appraisals
- Public market benchmarks

*These techniques don't work for startups; valuing startups is a black art.*

## A Better Way: Grounded in Market Realities

Need a systematic, detailed, objective and repeatable approach

- A framework grounded in market realities
- Make small but detailed, cumulative adjustments
- Use market data and real world norms

*When stacking a set of assumptions, start with what you know to be true or you will end up somewhere irrational.*

## Elements of a Realistic Valuation

"Founder Economics" need to work

Benchmarked against market-prevailing percent ownership norms

Must account for current market conditions

Must consider likely impact of future market conditions

Need recognition of importance of post-money and capital staging

*Things tend to revert toward the mean for a reason - valuations are constrained by the many issues they need to take into account.*

## Prevailing Ownership Norms

In 95% of angel deals (~70,000 US deals / year)

- Investors purchase 15-40% of the company
- And, in majority of deals, angels end up owning between 20% and 30% of company after seed round

*You can gain perspective on your deal by comparing it to prevailing norms.*

---

## Amount Raised Is Key Consideration

**$750K** investment @ **$2.25M** pre-money yields investors **25%**

**$1.0M** investment @ **$3.0M** pre-money yields investors **25%**

**$1.5M** investment @ **$4.5M** pre-money yields investors **25%**

**$2.0M** investment @ **$6.0M** pre-money yields investors **25%**

*Ask me about valuation and my first question will be about the size of the round. Every fraction has a numerator and a denominator.*

# Investor Psychology Matters

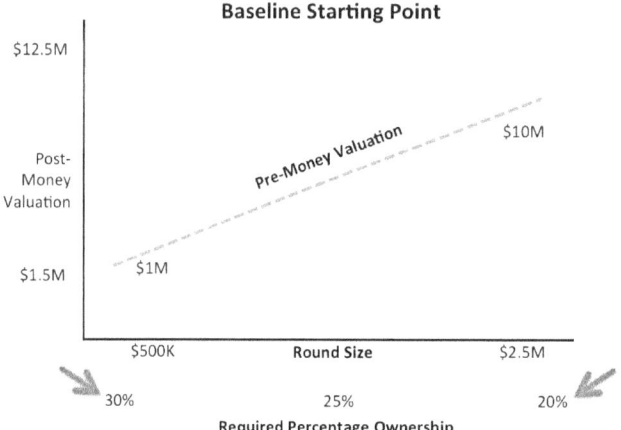

*As round size goes up, investors get comfortable owning less in percent terms (i.e. paying higher valuation).*

# Summary of the Seraf Method

Built on baseline percent ownership as a starting point - not as a goal, but as a yardstick

Then looks at raising or lowering from that starting point making adjustment in three key realms

1. Exit Realities
2. Financing Requirements
3. Current Deal Environment

*Specific ownership percentage doesn't matter to angels; it's just a way to compare a deal to market norms*

## Example Financing Requirements Adjustments
(see model for full set)

High margin business (e.g. software)  Low margin business (e.g. hardware)

Meaningful revenue now or soon  Long time to revenue

Short sales cycle  Long sales cycle

Inexpensive sales and distribution model  Direct sales, big inside sales

## Example Exit Reality Adjustments
(see model for full set)

Very big market (several billion TAM)  Small market (sub $200M TAM)

Fast growing market  Slow growing market

Obvious strategic buyers who will be threatened  No obvious strategic buyers to be threatened

Lots of strong, threatening IP  Little or no IP

# Example Deal and Environment Adjustments
(see model for full set)

Experienced, previously exited founding team  First time entrepreneurs

Product is complete and fully developed  Technical risk remains

Attractive deal structure, good deal terms  Investor unfriendly terms

Strong credible deal lead with good written diligence report  No strong deal lead, no diligence reports, "party round" with no one in charge

# Downloadable Model Allows Adjustments

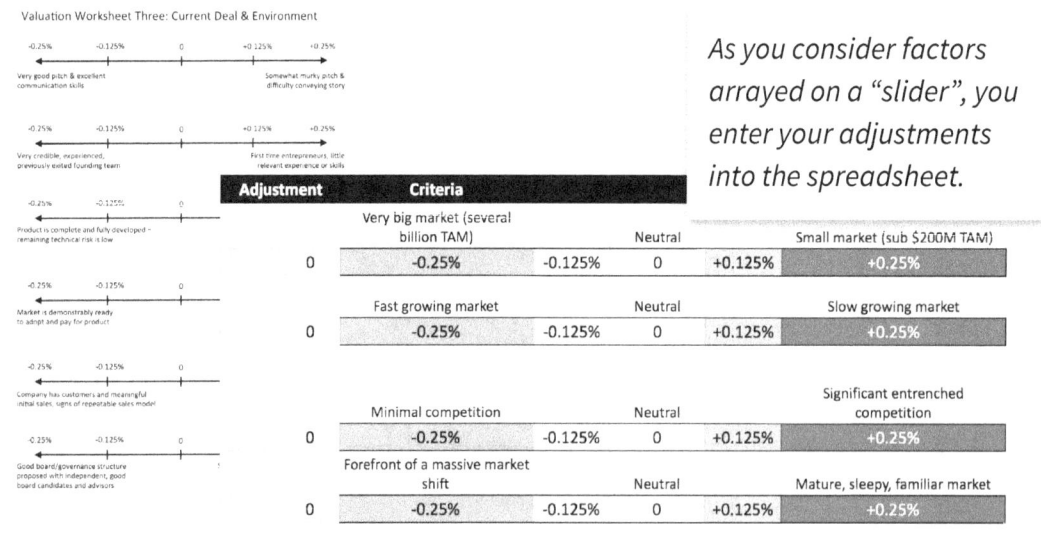

*As you consider factors arrayed on a "slider", you enter your adjustments into the spreadsheet.*

Downloadable Worksheet: https://bit.ly/DownloadValuationWorksheet

# Model Populates a Valuation Lookup Table

*Each of your adjustments carries forward and you can look up your adjusted valuation.*

| | |
|---|---|
| Adjustment Carried From Worksheet One | -0.250 |
| Adjustment Carried From Worksheet Two | -0.250 |
| Adjustment Carried From Worksheet Three | -0.375 |
| **Total Worksheet Four Adjustment** | **-0.00875** [Note: divided by 100 to make a percentage for calculation purposes] |

| ROUND SIZE | BASE PERCENT TO BE OWNED | ADJUSTED PERCENT OWNED | PRE- MONEY VALUATION | POST- MONEY VALUATION |
|---|---|---|---|---|
| $500,000 | 25.00% | 24.13% | $1,572,539 | $2,072,539 |
| $600,000 | 24.75% | 23.88% | $1,913,089 | $2,513,089 |
| $700,000 | 24.50% | 23.63% | $2,262,963 | $2,962,963 |
| $800,000 | 24.25% | 23.38% | $2,622,460 | $3,422,460 |
| $900,000 | 24.00% | 23.13% | $2,991,892 | $3,891,892 |
| $1,000,000 | 23.75% | 22.88% | $3,371,585 | $4,371,585 |
| $1,100,000 | 23.50% | 22.63% | $3,761,878 | $4,861,878 |

# INTRODUCTION TO ANGEL INVESTING
## Follow-On Theory

---

## What is a Follow-on Round?

Most fast-growing startups have a continuous need for funds to help grow the business

- "Follow-on" financings typically occur 9 to 15 months after prior round
- Investors can choose whether to participate or not in the new round

*Investing early in a company's history gives you a front row seat to observe how the company progresses and how the team executes.*

## To Follow-On or Not to Follow-On?

Active angels build large portfolios over time, resulting in regular requests for follow-on investments

Experienced angels reserve significant capital for follow-ons

It's not unusual for an angel to allocate 60%+ of their capital to follow-on rounds

*Over time, a successful portfolio allocation strategy will end up with more capital invested in the winners than in the losers!*

## Context Affects Follow-on Investments

With your first investment, you are buying an informational advantage

- As winners become apparent, make **offensive** investments to maintain your ownership
- For companies that struggle but still have potential, it may be necessary to make small **defensive** investments to protect your ownership

*It is all about building your position in the winners, but sometimes that requires writing checks when a company's fate is still not clear.*

## You Must Revisit Upside Potential

For strong companies, valuations tend to go up significantly with each financing round

With each new valuation, just like with your initial investment, you need to re-assess the three elements of valuation:

- Exit realities the company is facing
- Projected future financing requirements
- Deal particulars of this financing round

*It's up to you to look at the valuation factors in light of the new situation and determine whether the new valuation is attractive on a risk-adjusted basis.*

## Downside Risk Issues to Watch For

Here are some showstoppers that keep experienced angels from making additional investments:

- **Integrity issues** or concerns about honesty, transparency
- **Bad judgement** or poor decision-making on the part of the team
- **Board** is weak, not fully formed, not adding sufficient controls or value
- **Sales cycle** is longer than expected, **value prop** is weaker than expected or customer's **buying priority** is lower than expected
- Badly needed **key hires** were not made or are of low quality
- **Tech/Science** not turning out to be sufficiently promising

*Not every startup investment is going to work out. The ones with these attributes definitely won't work out.*

# INTRODUCTION TO ANGEL INVESTING
## Types of Exits

## Type of Exits

Both positive and negative exits come in different forms:

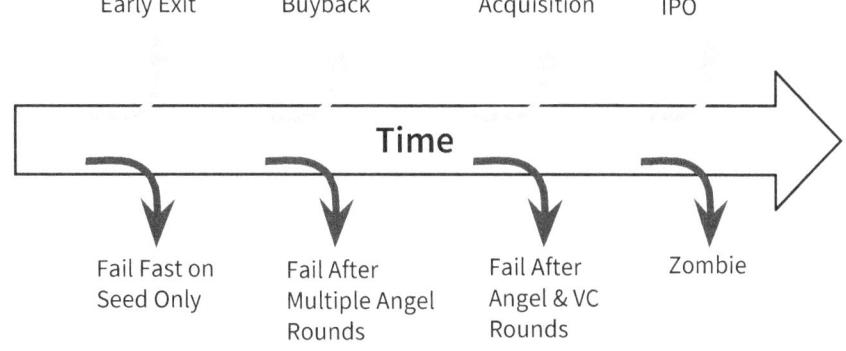

## Fail Fast on Seed Only

Usually characterized as an interesting idea that didn't pan out

Company raised small amount of capital, but:

- Product didn't work as expected, or
- Customers weren't that interested in buying, or
- Team didn't work well together

*Remember: the only thing worse than a mistake, is an expensive mistake.*

## Fail After Multiple Angel Rounds

Most common scenario for failed angel deals

- Company makes some early progress, but needs more capital
- One bridge round turns into two or three additional rounds
- Company continues to underachieve on business plan
- Investor fatigue sets in and company can't raise new financing
- The result is a fire sale of company's remaining assets

*This scenario highlights the human tendency to not want to admit you were wrong until absolutely forced to.*

## Fail After Angel and VC Rounds

Some of the most promising startups end up in this bucket

- You invest in seed round and company gets early traction
- VCs take interest and company raises Series A at good valuation
- Initial success doesn't pan out, growth stalls and company pivots
- New financing is needed resulting in heavy dilution to investors
- Company is sold at a modest price, returning little if any capital to early investors

*This is the kind of investment where having a careful follow-on decision making process can help your "average $ into winners" exceed your "average $ into losers."*

## Zombies

Most (if not all) experienced angels have at least one of these investments

- Business grows slowly but surely, revenues climb into low millions
- Company can stay in business - it is at or near cash flow breakeven
- But, it's too slow growing for VCs and too small for acquirers
- Founders aren't motivated to sell - they have a lifestyle company

*If you are an investor in a company that fits this description, get together with other investors and work with the CEO to come up with an exit plan.*

## Early Exits

Positive early exits happen when a company's new product:

- Complements a fast growing acquirer's product line
- Has potential to damage acquirer's market position
- Fills new emerging gap in acquirer's product line
- Has strategic patents acquirer can't risk going to a competitor

*Sometimes a double or triple is a great exit for you as long as it doesn't take too long to happen and the company has not raised too much.*

## Dividends and Royalties

Although relatively infrequent, dividends and royalties are a great way to generate returns

- It can take quite a while before a company has enough cash to fund a dividend payout
- Dividends can accumulate in the background; either simple or cummulative
- Royalty or Revenue-based payments are typically put in place as part of deal structure at the time of initial investment

*Revenue based financing provides early liquidity, but can harm growth. Dividends tend to hold management's feet to the fire as they shift value from common to preferred over time.*

## Stock Buy-outs and Buy-backs

Tend to come in two different flavors

- **Company** buys shares from investors interested in selling (buy-back)
  - Expect limited return to investors in this scenario

- New investor, typically a large VC, wants to buy more stock than company is willing to sell (buy-out)
  - New investor offers to buy shares from current investors

*Buy-backs come with slow-growing profitable companies; buy-outs come with rocket ships, and can be really tough "liquidity vs upside potential" decisions.*

## Large Acquisitions

By far the most common type of "big exit" for angels

- Expect will take many years since it takes time to build the kinds of things a major acquirer pays big money for
- Acquisition usually includes large payment and a smaller (10-25%) escrow payment 12 to 18 months in future

*Really big exits are much less common and can take many years of patient growth.*

## Successful IPOs

An IPO is the Holy Grail of angel investing

- IPOs are a rare beast these days
- Companies are staying private much longer and finding liquidity other ways
- Market for small IPOs is gone (for many reasons)
- Mezzanine funds, hedge funds, and private equity are active financiers for most, if not all, of a growing company's capital needs

*An IPO in your angel portfolio will not only give you awesome bragging rights for years to come, it will almost certainly ensure positive overall portfolio returns.*

# INTRODUCTION TO ANGEL INVESTING
## Angels and Taxes

## What US Tax Rules Apply to Angel Investing?

The key tax rules that offer significant benefits to US-based angels include:

- **Wins**: IRS Sections 1202 & 1045 provide benefits when you have capital gains
- **Losses**: IRS Section 1244 provides benefits when you have capital losses
- **Your Companies**: Huge R&D Tax credits available even to unprofitable companies - can be applied to payroll taxes

*IRS tax rules are subject to change. Make sure you have an accountant familiar with tax rules for investments in Qualified Small Business Stock (QSBS).*

## IRS Section 1202

Section 1202 allows for the exclusion of capital gains on stock

- You can exclude up to the greater of $10M or 10 times your investment
- You must hold the stock for at least 5 years

- Stock acquired between 8/10/93 and 2/17/09:  50% Exclusion
- Stock acquired between 2/18/09 and 9/27/10:  75% Exclusion
- Stock acquired after 9/28/10:  100% Exclusion

*Angels should make a 1202 & 1244 review a fixed part of every years tax checklist*

## IRS Section 1045

Section 1045 allows you to avoid paying capital gains if:

- You put all of your gains into a new QSBS investment
- You make the new investment within 60 days of the sale

The holding period of the new investment includes the holding period of the stock you just sold (helps with 1202)

*Be careful... don't let the tax tail wag the investment dog by jumping into an impulsive investment!*

## IRS Section 1244

This provision in the tax code comes into play on capital losses

In most situations, you will write off capital losses vs. your capital gains

However, Section 1244 allows you to write off losses vs. the higher earned income tax rate if you are part of the first $1M invested in a QSBS company

*Make sure you record whether you are part of the initial $1M invested in a company at time of investment. It can be very difficult to document this after a company goes out of business.*

# INTRODUCTION TO ANGEL INVESTING
## Appendix

## Resources - Model Deal Terms Summary Memo

Designed to give company founders a preview of how an investor thinks about deal terms so that there are no surprises and so that any potential "show-stoppers" can be identified and discussed before both sides put a lot of work into due diligence. This deal terms summary memo is intended as a guide to how an investor approaches their deal terms.

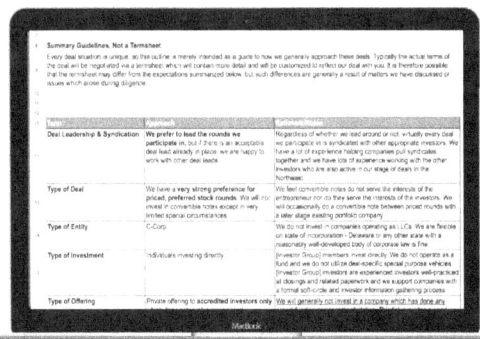

**Download Memo**
bit.ly/DealTermExpectations

## Resources - A Guide to Angel Investing Docs: Preferred Stock Deal

This guide is a quick overview of the principal documents in a fundraising where the investors are purchasing stock. These stock transactions permanently alter the capitalization of the company by adding new stockholders. Given this permanence and the associated complexity of these transactions, there are a great number of different types of deal documents used in stock transactions.

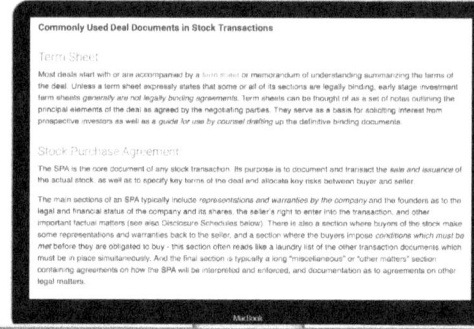

**Download Guide**
bit.ly/PreferredStockDocGuide

## Resources - A Guide to Angel Investing Docs: Convertible Debt Deal

This guide is intended to provide a quick overview and explanation of the principal documents in a fundraising where the investors are purchasing convertible debt. Unlike a stock transaction, these convertible debt deals do not alter the capitalization of the company by adding new stockholders until the debt is converted into equity. Compared to stock deals, there are a smaller number of types of deal documents used in convertible debt transactions.

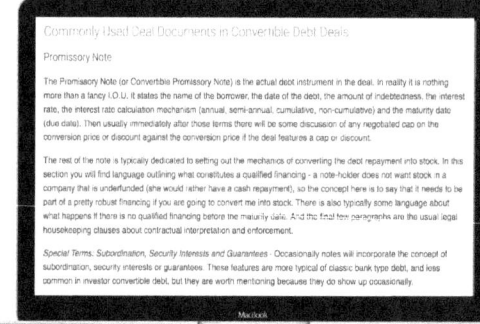

**Download Guide**
bit.ly/ConvertibleDebtDocGuide

# Resources - Sample Termsheet - Preferred Stock

This short simple example termsheet is intended to give a sense of what a very basic termsheet looks like. This particular example is called the Series Seed Termsheet v. 3.2 and is the work and property of the Series Seed project (www.seriesseed.com). Please review their SeriesSeed.com site for important information and disclaimers regarding use of this term sheet and its accompanying documents.

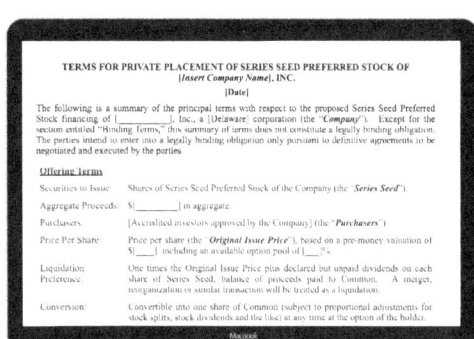

**Download Termsheet**
www.seriesseed.com

---

# Resources - Sample Termsheet - Convertible Note

This simple convertible note termsheet is intended to give readers a sense of what a very basic set of convertible note deal terms looks like. Readers should be advised that this particular example includes reference to a supplemental noteholders' agreement which is a separate contract to specify additional rights and obligations not included in a typical form of convertible note.

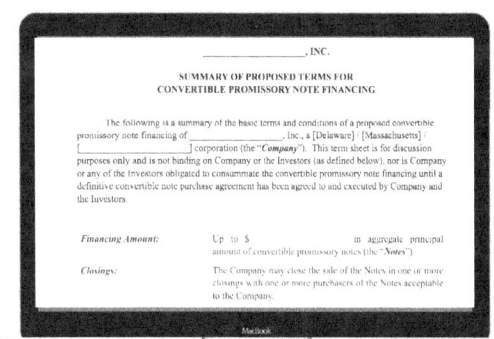

**Download Termsheet**
bit.ly/SampleConvNoteTermSheet

## Resources - Capitalization Tables with Waterfall Analysis

If you perform a Google search for the term "Cap Table", you will end up with dozens of tools to choose from. These options include everything from Excel spreadsheets that build simple cap tables all the way along the spectrum to complex, high-end software products. We built ones we think you might prefer.

1. We wanted a tool that was very simple to set up. We didn't want to have to enter lots of data to model a cap table.
2. We wanted a tool that allowed us to model a variety of different exit scenarios to help understand how much each shareholder would get depending on the size of the exit.
3. We wanted a tool that was free for everyone to use with no strings attached.

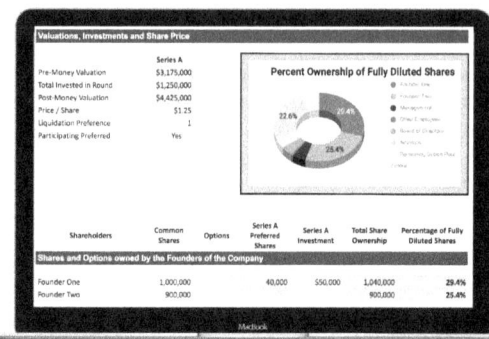

**Download Tool**
bit.ly/Series_A_and_B_Cap_Table_and_Waterfall

---

## Resources - Valuation Modeling Tool

This valuation modeling tool is designed to help investors determine a reasonable valuation for a potential investment based on market conditions for:

1. Exit Realities
2. Financing Requirements
3. Current Deal Environment

The Seraf Method for valuation revolves around the concept of percentage ownership because historical market norms allow us to use percentage ownership as a guideline or yardstick.

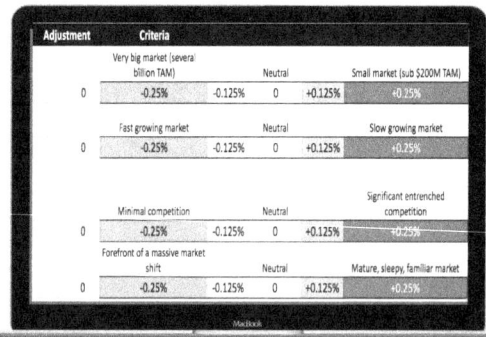

**Download Modeling Tool**
bit.ly/Seraf_Method_Valuations

# Resources - Exit Planning

Most early stage companies return maximum value to their shareholders through some form of acquisition. Planning for such an exit is an ongoing responsibility for both the CEO and the board. With that challenge in mind, we put together a guide to help with this planning exercise. CEOs should use this guide as an approach or checklist to help stay on top of who their potential acquirers are and what the company's relationship is with each acquirer. And, furthermore, CEOs should use this guide as a way to update the board on at least an annual basis.

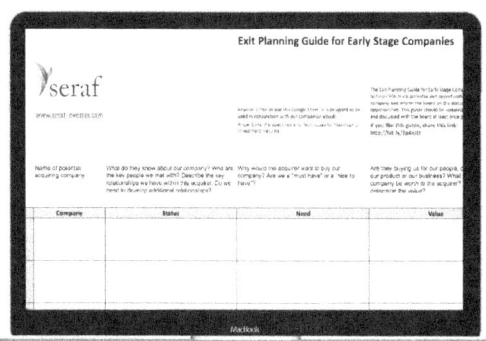

**Download Guide**
bit.ly/ExitPlanningGuide

# Continue Your Angel Education and Improve Your Investing Skills

The Seraf Compass guides early stage investors in making better investing decisions, minimizing risk and improving returns

**Introduction to Angel Investing Articles**
bit.ly/Angel201Articles

**Introduction to Angel Investing eBook**
bit.ly/Angel201eBook

**Introduction to Angel Investing Hardcopy Book**
bit.ly/HardCopyBooks

**Introduction to Angel Investing Tools**
bit.ly/SerafToolbox

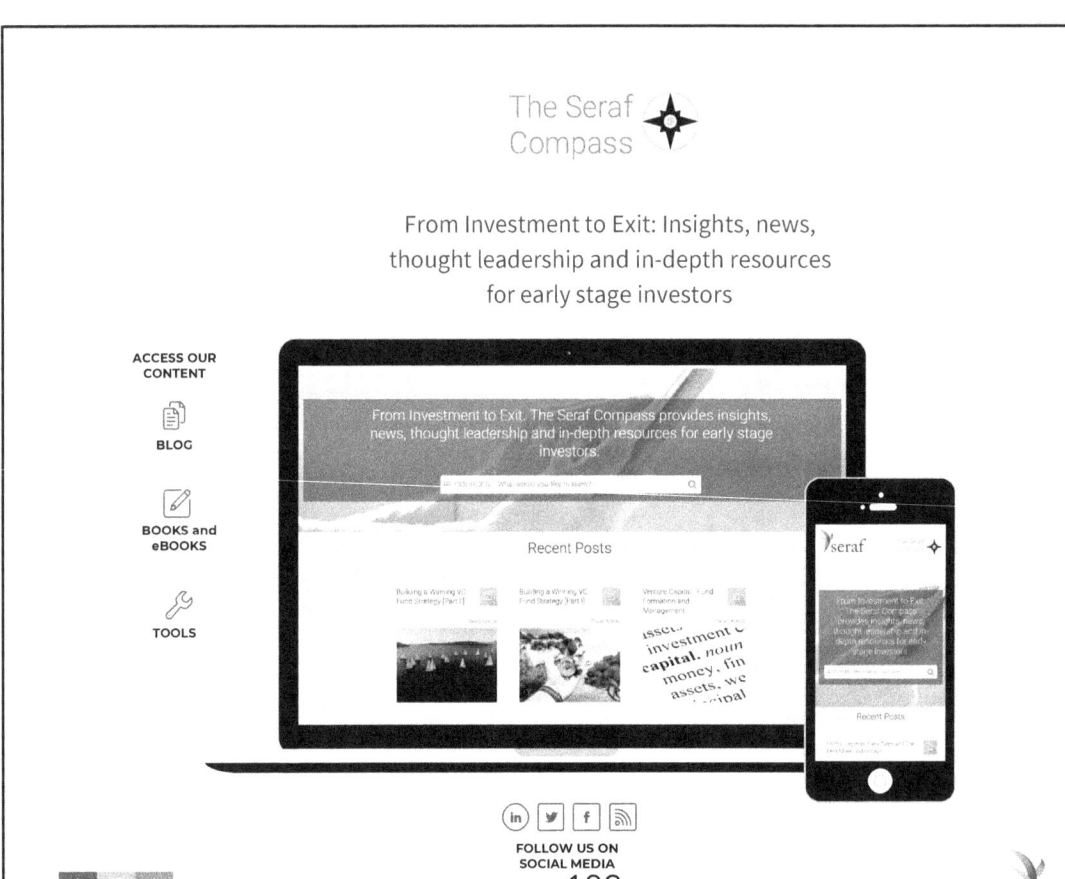

From Investment to Exit: Insights, news, thought leadership and in-depth resources for early stage investors

ACCESS OUR CONTENT

BLOG

BOOKS and eBOOKS

TOOLS

FOLLOW US ON SOCIAL MEDIA

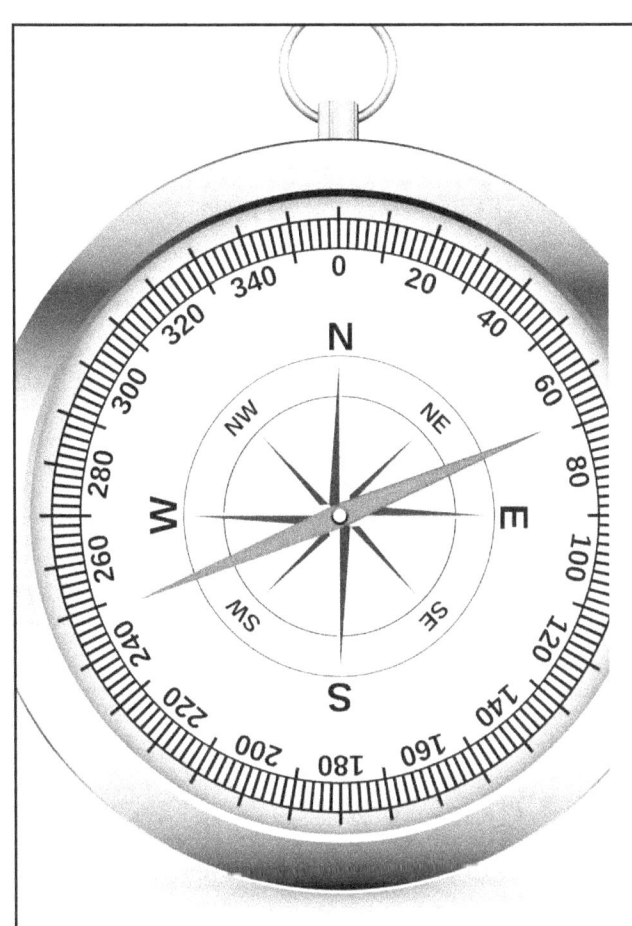

## Books from Seraf

### Fundamentals of Angel Investing
A Guide to the Principles, Skills and Concepts Every Angel Investor Needs to Succeed

### Angel Investing by the Numbers
Valuation, Capitalization, Portfolio Construction and Startup Economics

### Leaders Wanted: Making Startup Deals Happen
Advanced Techniques in Deal Leadership and Due Diligence for Early Stage Investors

### Guide, Advise and Inspire: How Startup Boards Drive Growth and Exits
An Overview of the Principles, Skills and Concepts Every Early Stage Company Board Member Needs to Succeed

### Venture Capital: A Practical Guide
A Guide to Fund Formation and Management

## PORTFOLIO MANAGEMENT FOR EARLY STAGE INVESTORS

All Your Info. One Place. Smart Investing

## WHAT MAKES SERAF DIFFERENT

**Easy Workflow**

Seraf guides you through a few easy steps to get your portfolio up and running quickly. Get an overview, develop insights and generate reports in no time.

**Deep Experience**

Designed by active, early stage investors with over 25 years experience in fund creation and management, the Seraf team understands the complexities of today's early stage investment landscape.

**Uniquely Focused Solution**

Developed specifically to meet the needs of early stage investors, Seraf provides the tools YOU need to manage your portfolio efficiently.

## AUTHORS

Hambleton Lord

Christopher Mirabile

## CONTACT US

www.seraf-investor.com

www.angelcapitalassociation.org

# Appendix

In this appendix, we provide a series of templates and guides to help improve your overall investment returns.

**Early Stage Investment Portfolio Modeling Tool**: This spreadsheet allows you to model potential outcomes for the overall return from an early stage investment portfolio. (https://bit.ly/Seraf_Portfolio_Modeling_Tool)

**Due Diligence Report**: This template is designed to result in a short, readable due diligence report. Our goal at Launchpad is to provide our investors with a 2 to 4 page summary report that is readable and comprehensive. It covers all the main areas in diligence and provides the author(s) with a structured approach. (http:/bit.ly/DueDiligenceReportTemplate)

**Due Diligence Checklist**: After reading this book, you might feel overwhelmed by all the different aspects in due diligence. The Due Diligence Checklist is designed as a quick reference guide to help steer you through the various aspects of diligence. (http:/bit.ly/Due_Diligence_Checklist)

**Customer Reference Check Questionnaire**: At the core of this questionnaire are a series of questions that will help you distinguish whether the company is selling aspirin, oxygen or jewelry. And, you can find out a bit more about the size of the potential market opportunity. (http:/bit.ly/CustomerReferenceChecks)

**Management Assessment Questionnaire**: This questionnaire is designed to get the story behind the CEO and his/her team. If you are able to make enough reference calls, you should be able to find similarities and differences to help you paint a pretty good picture of the team you are investing in. (http:/bit.ly/ManagementQuestionnaire)

**Guidelines for Successful Board Meetings**: Running a successful board meeting requires planning and discipline. Which in turn requires some experience and some guidelines. Without this preparation, you will waste precious time focusing on the wrong things. To help you orchestrate great board meetings, we pulled together a collection of well-tested guidelines that will make any early stage company board more productive. (http:/bit.ly/SuccessfulBoardMeetings)

**Model Deal Terms Summary Memo**: The purpose of this memo is to give companies a preview of how we think about deal terms so that there are no surprises and so that any potential "show-stoppers" can be identified and discussed before both sides put a lot of work into due diligence. (https://bit.ly/DealTermExpectations)

**A Guide to Angel Investing Docs - Preferred Stock Deal**: This guide is intended to provide a quick overview of the principal documents in a fundraising where the investors are purchasing stock. These stock transactions permanently alter the capitalization of the company by adding new stockholders, who are typically purchasing a brand new class of stock created for them, typically a series designated class of preferred stock with special rights and privileges they have negotiated.

**A Guide to Angel Investing Docs - Convertible Debt Deal**: This guide is intended to provide a quick overview and explanation of the principal documents in a fundraising where the investors are purchasing convertible debt. These convertible debt deals *do not alter the capitalization of the company by adding new stockholders until the debt is converted into equity.*

**Sample Termsheet - Preferred Stock**:  This short simple example termsheet is intended to give readers a sense of what a very basic termsheet looks like. This particular example is called the Series Seed Termsheet v. 3.2 and is the work and property of the Series Seed project (www.seriesseed.com).  Please review their SeriesSeed.com site for important information and disclaimers regarding use of this term sheet and its accompanying documents.

**Sample Termsheet - Convertible Note**:  This simple convertible note termsheet is intended to give readers a sense of what a very basic set of convertible note deal terms looks like. Readers should be advised that this particular example includes reference to a supplemental noteholders' agreement which is a separate contract to specify additional rights and obligations not included in a typical form of convertible note. (https://bit.ly/SampleConvNoteTermSheet)

**Valuation Modeling Tool**:  This valuation modeling tool is designed to help investors determine a reasonable valuation for a potential investment based on market conditions for:
1. Exit Realities
2. Financing Requirements
3. Current Deal Environment

The Seraf Method for valuation revolves around the concept of percentage ownership because historical market norms allow us to use percentage ownership as a guideline or yardstick. (https://bit.ly/Seraf_Method_Valuations)

**Capitalization Table with Waterfall Analysis**: This is a collection of two spreadsheets that help you model a company's capitalization table and the resulting waterfall analysis based on a variety of exit scenarios for the company. (https://bit.ly/Series_A_Cap_Table_and_Waterfall or https://bit.ly/Series_A_and_B_Cap_Table_and_Waterfall)

**Exit Planning Guide**: The startup company IPO is a much rarer creature than it used to be, so most early stage companies return maximum value to their shareholders through some form of acquisition. Planning for such an exit is an ongoing responsibility for both the CEO and the board. With that challenge in mind, we put together a guide to help with this planning exercise. (https://bit.ly/Exit_Planning_Guide)


Versions of each of these documents are available online. If you go to the URL next to each item, you will be able to access an online document that will save you time in creating your own copy of these documents.

# Early Stage Investment Portfolio Modeling Tool

One of the biggest challenges faced by early stage investors is to assemble a portfolio of investments that in aggregate return more than 2 times the original amount invested in the total portfolio. In the language of Venture Capital, the goal of a successful early stage investor is to achieve a Distributed to Paid-In (DPI) ratio greater than 2X. In other words, for every dollar you invest in your portfolio, you want to get two dollars back over time. And, if you want to be one of the top decile early stage investors, you want to shoot for a DPI of 3X or greater.

A successful early stage investment portfolio has a mix of strikeouts, base hits and home runs. So how is it possible for an early stage investor to build a successful portfolio compiled from companies that produce such widely different financial returns? To answer that question, we pulled together a simple modeling tool that helps you visualize how the probable returns play out and interact to produce an overall portfolio return. As usual, we built it as a Google Sheet that allows you to make a copy and model a number of scenarios for your own portfolio.

## Investment Portfolio

| | | | Type of Exit | Exit Multiple |
|---|---|---|---|---|
| Total Amount Invested | $500,000 | | Loss | 0 |
| Amount of Capital Returned | $1,335,000 | | Breakeven | 1 |
| Distributed to Paid-In (DPI) Capital Ratio | 2.67 | | Base Hit | 4 |
| | | | Home Run | 10 |
| | | | Grand Slam | 25 |

## Individual Investments: Exit Types and Returns

| Company Name | Total Investment | Percentage of Portfolio | Type of Exit | Total Amount Returned |
|---|---|---|---|---|
| Investment 1 | $25,000 | 5% | Loss | $0 |
| Investment 2 | $50,000 | 10% | Base Hit | $200,000 |
| Investment 3 | $25,000 | 5% | Loss | $0 |
| Investment 4 | $15,000 | 3% | Base Hit | $60,000 |
| Investment 5 | $50,000 | 10% | Home Run | $500,000 |
| Investment 6 | $25,000 | 5% | Loss | $0 |
| Investment 7 | $15,000 | 3% | Loss | $0 |
| Investment 8 | $50,000 | 10% | Breakeven | $50,000 |
| Investment 9 | $25,000 | 5% | Base Hit | $100,000 |
| Investment 10 | $25,000 | 5% | Breakeven | $25,000 |
| Investment 11 | $25,000 | 5% | Loss | $0 |
| Investment 12 | $50,000 | 10% | Base Hit | $200,000 |
| Investment 13 | $50,000 | 10% | Base Hit | $200,000 |
| Investment 14 | $20,000 | 4% | Loss | $0 |
| Investment 15 | $50,000 | 10% | Loss | $0 |
| Totals | $500,000 | 100% | | $1,335,000 |

How do you go about using this modeling tool? To start, we created a sample portfolio of 15 companies for you to work from. That's enough companies to begin with for a basic portfolio modeling exercise. For each company, there are two variables that you need to set.

- First, you will need to put in an **amount that you invest in each company**. In a portfolio of 15 companies, you might have the same amount invested in each company. Or, you might decide to distribute your investments in a less even fashion. In the default Google Sheet, we've set up a range of investment amounts. Some companies have as little as $15,000 invested and others have as much as $50,000.

- Second, you will need to chose or "model" the **type of exit for each company** in the portfolio. Here is where you determine the multiple of capital each company will return to your portfolio. Since we are dealing with early stage companies, you will have a real mix of returns. If you want a realistic model that will be predictive of probable real-life outcomes, we recommend that you set approximately half the portfolio to total losses (i.e. no capital returned). The rest of the portfolio can be a mix of moderate successes with maybe one or two bigger wins.

There is one other variable that you can control on this sheet. In the upper right quadrant of the sheet is a section for the Exit Multiple for each type of exit. We provide values for each exit type, but you might want to model using different exit multiples. So feel free to change these numbers to fit your needs.

Once you set the two variables for each company (and make any changes to the Exit Multiples), take a look in the upper left quadrant of the Google Sheet. There are three important metrics that are calculated for you in that section.

1. **Total Amount Invested**: This is the sum of all the investments you made in the portfolio and lists the total.

2. **Amount of Capital Returned**: This is the sum of all the returned capital based on the types of exits you set for each company.

3. **Distributed to Paid-In (DPI) Capital Ratio**: This represents the multiple of capital your portfolio returns. Remember, a solid DPI is 2 and a top quartile investor will have a DPI of 3 or greater.

As we discuss above, a DPI of 2X is a good target to aim for. And 3X is even better and puts you in league with the best VCs.

One final thought to keep in mind. This tool is helpful to determine your overall multiple of returned capital. However, it does not factor in the amount of time it took for this capital to be returned. As you are building your own early stage portfolio, make sure you watch out for how long it takes to get a return on your capital. If your returns take significantly more than 10 years to appear, your resulting IRR returns will be much less than optimal. You won't earn enough for the risk you are taking and you might be better off investing in the public stock markets!

# Due Diligence Report

This template is designed to result in a short, readable due diligence report. Our goal is to provide our investors with a 2 to 4 page summary report that is readable and comprehensive. It covers all the main areas in diligence and provides the author(s) with a structured approach.

**Company**: {Company Name}

**CEO**: {CEO Name}

**Report Date**: {Date}

**Company Description:**

{insert 1-2 paragraph summary description of company here}


**Due Diligence Assessment:**

{This section is the heart of the due diligence report. For each topic, we provide you with example questions that make for appropriate areas to discuss in the remarks column. This report template is deliberately designed as a table to force the authors to be concise. It's important to be succinct in your diligence findings summary. Otherwise, you will end up with a long report that investors won't read through, thus defeating the purpose of the report. If you have important detail or documents that you feel must be included in your findings, you can make them into appendices and refer to them in the report, but can be a slippery slope toward an excessively long package. A better approach is to keep primary research materials and memos in a cloud folder you can make available to the minority of investors who want more detail.}

| Topic | Rating | Remarks |
|---|---|---|
| Investment Thesis | | |
| What Needs To Be Believed (WNTBB) | | |
| Failure Risk | | |
| Leadership Assessment | | |
| Technology, IP and Product Roadmap | | |
| Customer Need and Go-To-Market Plan | | |
| Uniqueness and Competition | | |
| Market Size and Market Opportunity | | |
| Financial Projections and Funding Strategy | | |
| Exit Strategy | | |
| Deal Terms and Payoff | | |

**Individual Assessments:**

{This section of the report is designed to allow each member of the due diligence team to provide some short feedback on their personal opinion of the investment opportunity. You shouldn't expect everyone's assessment to be positive. In fact, it's important to have at least one or two dissenting opinions to add balance to the report. And, make sure to ask for succinct summary comments. It is especially helpful if each commenter ends their comments with a note about whether they plan to invest and why/why not.}

| Team Member | Rating | Summary Remarks |
|---|---|---|
| {Name 1} | | |
| {Name 2} | | |
| {Name 3} | | |

**Key**

(++) = Very Positive (+) = Positive (0) = Neutral

(–) = Negative but issues can be overcome

( / ) Very Negative, issues cannot be overcome

**Investment Thesis:** This section is where you explain the overall logic of the investment and characterize how it is that investors will make money. Questions you may want to cover here include:

- Is this a billion dollar IPO opportunity or is it more likely to be acquired for under $50M? Or something in between?
- Are there limited number of risks that can be mitigated or is this a moonshot deal with big risk and potentially big reward?
- Will it take 10 years to complete the product and get FDA approval, or could this company be acquired in the first couple of years by a big competitor?

**What Needs to Be Believed (WNTBB):** This section is where you boil down all of the key risks that need to be assumed in order to invest (see companion eBook for more detail). If an investor cannot make peace with or cannot believe an item on this list can be overcome, she should not invest. Example WNTBBs might include:

- That this market can be disrupted.
- That enough customers will find this essential at this price point.
- That the company will be successful in transitioning from current niche to mainstream.
- That the company can build out a successful go to market plan and demonstrate traction on this round size.
- That this management team can scale to pull this off.
- That the company can achieve market share before the large competitors crowd them out.

**Failure Risk:** This section is where you talk about the main weaknesses in the plan and the degree to which they are mitigated. If this company fails is it likely for lack of capitalization, inability to make the technology work, competition?

**Leadership Assessment:** This section is where you discuss your assessment of the management team. Questions you may want to cover here include:

- Does the CEO possess the experience and leadership abilities to succeed?
- Do they have skills for where they are going, as opposed to where they have been?
- Do the CEO and team have a proven track record?

- Does the team possess the appropriate balance of experience and skill sets?
- Are the board members and advisors suitable and committed?
- What key hires are needed to address gaps?

**Technology, IP and Product Roadmap**: This section is where you discuss your assessment of the technology and technology risk as well as the IP situation. Questions you may want to cover here include:

- Is the technical team qualified and experienced?
- How strong are the technology and IP positions?
- Is there a product roadmap and is it achievable?
- What are the remaining risks related to technology, IP and product roadmap?
- Are their superior technologies on the near term horizon?

**Customer Need and Go-To-Market Plan**: This section is where you discuss your assessment of the plan to take the product to market. Questions you may want to cover here include:

- Is the GTM plan sufficiently detailed?
- Are the assumptions, including required level of sales spend and time lines reasonable?
- Is the sales pipeline adequate, and are key metrics for adoption rate, conversion rates, etc. conservative?
- Do customers confirm the need and likely adoption rates?
- Beyond verifying some demand, do we understand the customers buying priorities? Is this Oxygen, Aspirin or Jewelry?
- What are the major risks in marketing awareness, customer adoption rates and sales cycle?

**Uniqueness and Competition**: This section is where you discuss your assessment of the overall competitiveness and defensibility of the offering. Questions you may want to cover here include:

- Is the company well positioned with respect to current and likely future competitors?
- Is the founding team well-informed about their market and industry? Do they have a good competitive sense, or are they unaware of key issues?

- What are the major risks in marketing awareness, customer adoption rates and sales cycle?

**Market Size and Market Opportunity**: This section is where you discuss your assessment of the actual addressable market. Questions you may want to cover here include:

- Are the top-down and bottoms-up market estimates consistent and attractive?
- Are the market share projections reasonable?
- What are the remaining risks in market development?

**Financial Projections and Funding Strategy**: This section is where you discuss your assessment of the financial plan and capital raising strategy. Questions you may want to cover here include:

- Does the balance sheet make sense, and are there any showstopper issues?
- Are the financial projections reasonable and conservative in light of past performance?
- What are the implications of variances in key assumptions?
- Is the future financing risk manageable?
- What are remaining financial risks?
- Are the assumptions about scaling expense (e.g. G&A, etc.) reasonable, or is the model unrealistic?

**Exit Strategy**: This section is where you discuss your assessment of the likely exit opportunities. Questions you may want to cover here include:

- Is there alignment with the CEO and team on exit goals?
- Is the exit strategy reasonable?
- Is the assumed timeline reasonable?
- What exit multiples can be predicted under representative scenarios?
- Does the CEO know people in the industry? Is he/she a networker who will make the relationships and do the thought-leadership necessary to get a buyer interested?

**Deal Terms and Payoff**: This section is where you summarize the relationship between the deal terms in the termsheet and the expected investor return. Questions you may want to cover here include:

- Is this a low valuation, high risk deal, or a high valuation, low risk deal?
- Does the termsheet include specific terms intended to protect this round of investors?
- Can you show the desired return multiple based on exit multiples for comparable companies?

# Due Diligence Checklist

This checklist is designed to be appropriate for early stage investments. The "Information Request" and "Tasks" columns list those items and tasks, respectively, that are generally required, at a minimum, to complete diligence. The "Key Questions" column is representative of typical questions the diligence effort should address. The information request, tasks, and key questions should all be reviewed and revised, as needed, for the particular situation. The "Summary Points" column may be used by the team to summarize the answers to key questions in preparation for drafting the diligence report. Thank you to Launchpad member Gail Greenwald for her help developing this checklist.

# Leadership Assessment

| Information Request | Tasks | Key Questions |
|---|---|---|
| Resumes for key leadership team members | Review resumes | Does the CEO possess the experience and leadership abilities to succeed? |
| Professional references for key team members | Interview references (see interview guidelines) | Do they have skills for where they are going, as opposed to where they have been? |
| Resumes and contact info for board members and advisors | Gather additional information from network as available (asking around, checking LinkedIn - anything to find blind reference checks) | Do the CEO and team have a proven track record? |
| | Assign team member(s) to spend time with CEO | Does the team possess the appropriate balance of experience and skill sets? |
| | Assess CEO and team for leadership, integrity, track record, required competencies | Are the board members and advisors suitable and committed? |
| | Assess suitability and commitment of board members and advisors | What key hires are needed to address gaps? |

# Technology, IP and Product Roadmap

| Information Request | Tasks | Key Questions |
|---|---|---|
| Descriptions of technology and product | Review information and meet with technical team | Is the technical team qualified and experienced? |
| Relevant technical publications | Assess critical technologies, tool choices, software architecture choices, scalability of solution | How strong are the technology and IP positions? |
| Patents and patent applications | Assess IP defensibility | Is the product roadmap achievable? |
| Related IP info (defense: Freedom to Operate (FTO)?, offense: enforceability?) | Conduct additional secondary research as needed | What are the remaining risks related to technology, IP and product roadmap? |
| Product roadmap with key milestones | Conduct additional expert interviews if needed | Are their superior technologies on the near term horizon? |
| Competing technologies and commercialization status | Assess remaining technical risk, IP defensibility, competitive technical position | |

# Regulatory Strategy

| Information Request | Tasks | Key Questions |
|---|---|---|
| Regulatory strategy, if relevant | Review regulatory strategy | Is the regulatory strategy well thought through and feasible? |
| Status of dialogue with regulatory authorities and/or consultants, copies of relevant communications | Interview regulatory experts | Are the company's financial resources sufficient to implement the regulatory plan? |
| | Assess comparable regulatory pathways for other products as appropriate | Are assumptions about partners/acquirers' roles in the regulatory plan reasonable? |
| | Assess regulatory climate | What are the remaining regulatory risks? |

# Customer Need and Go-to-Market Plan

| Information Request | Tasks | Key Questions |
|---|---|---|
| Go-to-market plan with key milestones and granular detail on sales approach | Review information and meet with marketing and sales team | Is the GTM plan reasonable? |
| Partner identification and relationship status | Interview customers, partners, prospects as appropriate | Is the sales pipeline adequate, and are key metrics for adoption rate, conversion rates, etc. conservative? |
| Sales pipeline by stage, factored to be truly realistic and achievable | Gather information on industry comparisons as appropriate | Do customers confirm the need and likely adoption rates? |
| Any current marketing, joint venture, distribution agreements | Collaborate with financial team to assess revenue and pricing model | Beyond verifying some demand, do we understand the customers buying priorities? Is this Oxygen, Aspirin or Jewelry? |
| Customer, prospect, and partner references (see guidelines for interviewing customers) | | What are the major risks in marketing awareness, customer adoption rates and sales cycle? |

# Uniqueness and Competition

| Information Request | Tasks | Key Questions |
|---|---|---|
| List of current and prospective competitors | Gather additional competitive intelligence as needed | Is the company well positioned with respect to current and likely future competitors? |
| Competitive analysis including market share, relative strengths and weaknesses | Assess competitive environment, competitor positions, barriers to entry | Is the founding team well-informed about their market and industry? Do they have a good competitive sense, or are they unaware of key issues? |
| | | What are the major risks in marketing awareness, customer adoption rates and sales cycle? |

## Customer Reference Check Questionnaire

At the core of this questionnaire are a series of questions that will help you distinguish whether the company is selling aspirin, oxygen or jewelry. And, you can find out a bit more about the size of the potential market opportunity.

| **Customer Reference Check Questionnaire** |
|---|
| What are the reasons for purchasing company's products/services? What problem does this product/service solve for you? |
| Is this product a "Need to Have" or a "Nice to Have" for your organization? |
| What are your expectations / goals for this (e.g. improved revenue, reduced costs, etc.)? |
| Does the ROI for this product justify the current pricing? Would you expect to pay more or less for the product? |
| Have you used similar products/services before? |
| On your list of the top problems in your organization, where does solving this problem fall on your priority list? |
| Is your company generally an early or late adopter of new solutions? |
| Which products/services from the company do you use? Do you expect to add additional products/services in the future? |
| Did you look at any competitive products? |
| Why did you select company over other competitors? |
| As a customer/prospect for (company's) products/services, how did your interaction with the company go? Did they meet your expectations? |
| What is your impression of the company's management team? |

## Management Assessment Questionnaire

This questionnaire is designed to get the story behind the CEO and his/her team. If you are able to make enough reference calls, you should be able to find similarities and differences to help you paint a pretty good picture of the team you are investing in.

## Management Assessment Questionnaire

What are {CEO Name's} strengths?

What are some areas for further development?

What's the best way to tell {CEO Name} something you know he/she doesn't want to hear?

How does {CEO Name} use advisors? Does he/she share everything and ask for reaction, or does he/she just come with specific (e.g. narrow questions / concerns?) How open is he/she to influence from advisors (e.g. investors?)

If {Company Name} were to fail due to leadership, it would be because of what characteristic of {CEO Name}?

Does {CEO Name} show sufficient emotional intelligence to be able to navigate the typical ups and downs of an early stage company?

Do one or more members of the management team have a proven track record and does prior track record include successful exit(s)/returned money to investors?

Does the management team have applicable domain expertise?

Does the management team have complementary skills?

# Guidelines for Successful Board Meetings

Running a successful board meeting requires planning and discipline. Which in turn requires some experience and some guidelines. Without this preparation, you will waste precious time focusing on the wrong things. To help you orchestrate great board meetings, we pulled together a collection of well-tested guidelines that will make any early stage company board more productive. Key areas include:

- Topics you should cover in a company's first board meeting
- A high level agenda for regular board meetings
- Typical board calendar structure for early stage companies
- An overview of the package of materials that are sent out in advance of a board meeting
- An outline for a quarterly report to all investors.

**First Board Meeting Agenda**

For many startup companies, you will join a board that has limited structure to both the meetings and other key governance issues. Make sure that best practices for boards are put in place early on. We recommend that the initial board meeting use the following agenda.

- Appoint Secretary (usually company lawyer), Assistant Secretary (someone to sign documents) and Secretary pro tem (writes minutes)
- Discuss appointing a Chair or Lead Director (best practice) or none (absence can lead to dysfunction over time)
- Discuss use of company lawyer at board meetings (it can be very valuable and most lawyers will attend board meetings for free or at a very significant discount)
- Adopt stock option plan and new bylaws
- Appoint audit and compensation committees (all independent directors)
- Establish board meeting calendar for the next 6 to 12 months
- Establish standard agenda for first few meetings
- Authorize purchase of D&O Insurance
- Approve budget for first round of financing and/or year

## Creating a Board Calendar

Setting an appropriate level of board meetings is not that complicated. Young companies need a bit more regular oversight than more mature companies. That said, you don't want to have the company CEO spending too much of her time prepping for board meetings and not focusing on moving the company forward. A structure we use with many of our portfolio companies is based on the following 8 meetings a year tempo.

- Full board meeting once a quarter where everyone attends in person. These meetings tend to last 3 to 4 hours.
- Phone call status meetings halfway between the quarterly meetings. These meetings tend to last 1 to 2 hours. Please note that these call in meetings are more productive if done with video conferencing. Board members tend to stay more focused when they know you can see their face!

Another best practice to help build board cohesiveness is to hold a dinner the night before the board meeting. This dinner shouldn't focus on topics related to the company. Instead, it's an opportunity for board members to get to know each other and help build the bonds needed to get the company through good times and bad.

## Standard Board Meeting Agenda

Use a standard format for each of your regular board meetings – Most early stage companies will want to use the following format for their board meeting structure:

1) **Introduction**: This part of the meeting should take 30 minutes or less.
   - Handle housekeeping issues such as approving minutes, option grants, etc.
   - Review of the management dashboard.

2) **Strategic Discussion**: This is the core of the meeting and will take up the majority of the meeting time.
   - This is where the board "earns its keep" in terms of adding business value. Helping the company address key strategic issues in areas such as product, market, team, competition and funding are what an early stage board is supposed to do.

3) **Function Review**: This is more of a report and a minority of meeting time is allocated to it.
   - Invite the management team to provide an update on each department (or bring in one department per meeting for a deeper dive)
   - Key department discussions include: R&D, Sales, Marketing and Finance
   - Provide board interaction with the management team and give them a sense of how the board thinks and how they are held accountable by the board.

4) **Executive Session**: This special session typically occurs after the end of the main meeting, paradoxically, and refers to a session where the executives (including the CEO) are out of the room. It is a good practice to hold an Executive Session even if there is nothing special to discuss, because it can be very unsettling to a CEO to have one called when they are not the norm.
   - Gives independent board members a chance to discuss the whole management team in confidence.
   - Board Chair or lead director will typically be instructed to circle back to the CEO on the executive session, and there should be consensus or even explicit instructions on what to say if the topic is sensitive – many misunderstandings are born from inaccurately summarized executive sessions.
   - This is a good time to discuss key topics that the independent board members would like to have the CEO cover at the next board meeting.

Overview of a Board Reporting Pack

There are several items that most board packs have in common. You should typically expect to find four different sets of documents:
- Meeting Agenda,
- Minutes from prior board meetings,
- Financials, and
- Slide deck with key strategic discussion topics and company status update.

Directors should read these materials in advance of the board meeting and come prepared with any clarifying questions and comments.

- **Meeting Agenda** – This document should be one page long, and should not make any reference to the length of discussions.
- **Board Minutes** – This document should be a very short and concise summary of the last board meeting and contain the list of meeting attendees and any votes acted on by the board.
- **Financials** – This set of spreadsheets should include the company's Profit & Loss Statement, Balance Sheet and Cash Flow Statement. It is also useful to have current vs. plan comparisons. It should include a forecast at least for the remainder of the year.
- **Key Discussion / Company Status** – In most cases this will be a PowerPoint deck with 15 to 30 slides. The slide deck should include: 1) repeat of meeting agenda, 2) board actions, 3) management dashboard, 4) key strategic issues for discussion, and 5) a brief status update on/from each department.

**Quarterly Update for Investors**

Quarterly reports are essential for keeping investors in the loop and limiting surprises. They should be 2-3 pages long and include quarterly financials. Since many CEOs don't have experience writing them, the following list is a useful outline for composing quarterly reports:

- Brief discussion describing progress made since the last update
- Include info on Product, Team, Competition, Partnerships
- Brief discussion of key current challenges
- Financial performance highlighting recent sales and operational expenses
- Update on cash position and plans for future fund-raising
- Where appropriate, make sure to ask the investors for help in areas where their network can be of service to the company (e.g. referrals into target customers / partners, referrals for key new hires, etc.)
- Depending on the number of investors it might make sense to send a forecast
- Requests for help from the investors (e.g. referrals into target customers / partners, referrals for key new hires, etc.)
- Include recent P&L, Balance Sheet and Cash Flow reports

# Model Deal Terms Summary Memo

At Launchpad, we invest in dozens of companies every year. In the past, we frequently faced situations where we put a lot of work into diligence with a company and suddenly found out we were miles apart on deal term expectations and couldn't close the gap. This is a waste of time for all involved, and is the kind of frustration that leads to "deal fatigue" for investors trying to build a portfolio of investments. It can also lead to bad feelings and an increasing sense of mistrust between investors and entrepreneurs.

A good way to avoid this issue is try to be more explicit about what your deal term expectations are early on in your discussions with the entrepreneur. Once you have tried to do that off the cuff a couple times, you quickly see the value of having a written outline of your expectations. At Launchpad, we have been using a written outline for a while and we found it has helped a great deal. As the leaders of a network of investors, we see ourselves as managing a finite "human capital budget," and so anything that avoids wasted effort allows us to redirect those valuable cycles to other more important tasks.

Every deal situation is unique, so this memo is merely intended as a guide to how we generally approach these deals. Typically the actual terms of the deal will be negotiated via a termsheet which will contain more detail and will be customized to reflect our deal with the company. It is therefore possible that the termsheet may differ from the expectations summarized below, but such differences are generally a result of matters we have discussed or issues which arose during diligence.

| Term | Approach | Rationale / Notes |
|---|---|---|
| Deal Leadership & Syndication | **We prefer to lead the rounds we participate in,** but if there is an acceptable deal lead already in place, we are happy to work with other deal leads. | Regardless of whether we lead around or not, virtually every deal we participate in is syndicated with other appropriate investors. We have a lot of experience helping companies pull syndicates together and we have lots of experience working with the other investors who are also active in our stage of deals in New England. |
| Type of Deal | We have a **very strong preference for priced, preferred stock rounds**. We will not invest in convertible notes except in very limited special circumstances. | We feel convertible notes do not serve the interests of the entrepreneur nor do they serve the interests of the investors. We will occasionally do a convertible note between priced rounds with a later stage existing portfolio company. |
| Type of Entity | C-Corp. | We do not invest in companies operating as LLCs. We are flexible on state of incorporation - Delaware or any other state with a reasonably well-developed body of corporate law is fine. |
| Type of Investment | Individuals investing directly. | [Investor Group] members invest directly. We do not operate as a fund and we do not utilize deal-specific special purpose vehicles. [Investor Group] investors are experienced investors well-practiced at closings and related paperwork and we support companies with a formal soft-circle and investor information gathering process. |
| Type of Offering | Private offering to **accredited investors only** which does not involve any general solicitation and which complies with Rule 506(c). | We will generally not invest in a company which has done any crowd-funding or general solicitation. This link provides a good backgrounder on Rule 506(c). We also expect the company to give a representation that it is a Qualified Small Business under IRS rules. |

| Term | Approach | Rationale / Notes |
|---|---|---|
| Size of Round | We take a **collaborative approach** working with you to agree on round size, but strongly encourage companies to raise enough to ensure they can reach the next meaningful milestone. | Most rounds are undersized and most companies get into trouble by signing up for all the implications of a particular post-money valuation, but don't have sufficient resources to grow into that post money valuation. We also encourage companies to be a little bit flexible about accepting a few dollars extra if there is a bit more interest in the round than originally anticipated. |
| Pre-Money Valuation | We invest in deals with a **pre-money valuation which equates to 20-28% collective post money ownership** of the company by round participants. Where risk factors and capital intensity are lower, we will go lower in that range and where risk factors and capital intensity are higher, we will expect to be higher in that range. | Our expectations for valuation are based on our experience and market norms for the ~70,000 early stage deals which have been done each year in the US over the last decade. Note that round size plays a major role in determining pre-money valuation; for example, a $1M raise on a $3M pre-money equates to 25% post-money ownership, but so does $1.5M on $4.5M, $2M on $6M and $750K on $2.25M. This link provides a good backgrounder on how we think about valuation. |
| Board Composition | We expect you to form a **proper balanced corporate board of 5 people** consisting of 2 founders, 2 investors and 1 independent industry expert. We also request an observer slot - the observer has no vote or formal role, but is there as an understudy for our director as well as an extra source of connections or advice. | Boards are a bit of work, but they provide tremendous value for early stage teams by serving as a sounding board and source of strategic thinking and advice. Once a company has raised a significant amount of money from outsiders a proper board is also a necessity for proper fiduciary management and to protect against liability for the founding team. For companies going on to raise VC, our expectation is that one or more of the angel investor seats may be surrendered to the VCs to maintain the same size board. |

| Term | Approach | Rationale / Notes |
|---|---|---|
| Option Pool | We take a **collaborative approach** working with you to agree on the right size for the pre-money option pool. Generally you are looking to "fund" the hiring plan for the period of time covered by the round. | In our experience, an option pool large enough to equate to about 10% of the post-money capitalization is plenty, but there can be situations where a bit less or a bit more is appropriate. |
| Type of Security | The name of the security doesn't matter to us - "Series Seed Preferred," "Series Seed 1 Preferred," "Series A Preferred," "Series Angel," "Series 1 Preferred" etc. are all fine. | You pick. If you don't have a preference, let's call it Series 1 Preferred or Series Angel 1 Preferred to avoid some of the baggage associated with "seed round" or "Series A Round" |
| Liquidation Preference | **Participating preferred** with a **1X** liquidation preference. Participating preferred is paid back 1X before converting to common, HOWEVER, **we utilize a sunset clause** which reverts it to plain preferred in the event of an "up round" so that the term does not affect later rounds. | We have an expectation that you are trying to build a big company. A small early positive exit, while tempting, should only happen if you believe the bigger opportunity isn't there. This term aligns our incentives for that by providing a little bit of return to us for small positive exits where only our money is involved, but the term disappears if you raise a subsequent round of financing. Our approach is admittedly somewhat unique. It is meant to be a balanced and fair solution: it doesn't change the economics in a failure or a big win, but it does prevent a fast mediocre outcome that amounts to a zero interest loan from us to you. If things go well, our participation element goes away as if it never existed. |

| Term | Approach | Rationale / Notes |
|---|---|---|
| Dividends | We **generally do NOT ask for a dividend**, though we might in certain situations, and if we do, we typically keep it on the low side in the 4-6% range. | The most likely scenario in which we'd look at a dividend is a situation where we perceive a heightened risk of a "lifestyle company" sort of outcome. When we use them, they are accruing non-cumulative dividends payable at the time of exit or when other dividends are issued. |
| Anti-Dilution | We look for typical vanilla **broad-based weighted average** anti-dilution protection. | This is the near universal standard and is intended to minimize and contain the effect of any re-pricing while still being somewhat fair to earlier investors. |
| Drag-Along | We look for a provision stating that in a change of control situation, where a **majority of common and preferred agree to the deal**, the minority will go along and sign the documents. | The purpose of this kind of clause is to avoid a situation where an opportunity to sell the company is lost because a small minority causes much delay and confusion and the market moment passes and the buyer loses interest. If the majority thinks it is a good idea, then it is time to move. |
| ROFR & Co-Sale Rights | Company and investors have a **right of first refusal to buy shares sold by insiders**, and if they don't want them, then they have a **right to be part of the sale**. | This is about controlling who the investors are if an investor is leaving and about sharing in liquidity if things are not going well. Insider transfers are restricted and rare enough that it is uncommon for these clauses to be used, but they are a standard preferred stock investing term and they are reasonable and unobjectionable. |
| Redemption Rights | We **generally do not include a redemption rights window** in our deals. | These can be a little heavy-handed and are typically associated with closed-end funds, but they are coming back into style in the angel space due to exit concerns and we reserve the right to change our mind on this at some future date. |

150

| Term | Approach | Rationale / Notes |
|---|---|---|
| Registration Rights | We **generally do not include IPO registration rights** in our deals, but chose instead to say if anyone gets them later, we get them too. | IPOs are unfortunately so uncommon these days and are typically associated with companies which go so far beyond the angel stage that it doesn't make a lot of sense to negotiate them at our stage. |
| Founder Vesting | We will expect to have a **meaningful portion of the stock of key founders subject to contractual clawback restrictions which lapse over time.** | We look to be reasonable and collaborative here based on the company situation, but the concern we need to address is the unexpected departure of a founder who takes a huge chunk of the cap table with her/him. Not only is this very dilutive in terms of stock lost, but also there is big dilution associated with replacement. Further, it can result in a dissident shareholder with a massive voting block. That possibility can make for a very unattractive investment, hence the effort to try and claw some back in those situations. |
| Information Rights | We look for very **standard information rights**: annual financials, quarterly or monthly management reports. We don't necessarily insist on audited financials, but do request accountant/auditor review them. | Information rights help you keep your investors engaged and assisting you. We <u>strongly</u> discourage trying to limit information rights to major investors, however if you do, we will need you to stipulate that [Investor Group] is a major investor. |
| Pro-Rata Rights | We look for standard pro-rata rights to invest in future rounds to maintain our pro-rata interest. | Pro-Rata rights help you keep your investors engaged and assisting you. Follow-on investing is how experienced angels make their portfolios successful. We <u>strongly</u> discourage trying to limit pro-rata rights to major investors, however if you do, we will need you to stipulate that [Investor Group] is a major investor; we will not invest without pro-rata rights. |

# A Guide to Angel Investing Docs - Preferred Stock Deal

Given this permanence and the associated complexity of Preferred Stock transactions, there are a great number of different types of deal documents used in these deals. For the purposes of clarity, we've divided them into Commonly Used and Occasionally Used. Readers should also keep in mind that this guide talks in generalities in terms of where concepts are typically covered - every deal is different and a given issue may be addressed by counsel in a different way or in a different document in your deal.

# Commonly Used Deal Documents in Stock Transactions

## Term Sheet
Most deals start with or are accompanied by a term sheet or memorandum of understanding summarizing the terms of the deal. Unless a term sheet expressly states that some or all of its sections are legally binding, early stage investment term sheets *generally are not legally binding agreements*. Term sheets can be thought of as a set of notes outlining the principal elements of the deal as agreed by the negotiating parties. They serve as a basis for soliciting interest from prospective investors as well as a *guide for use by counsel drafting* up the definitive binding documents.

## Stock Purchase Agreement
The SPA is the core document of any stock transaction. Its purpose is to document and transact the *sale and issuance* of the actual stock, as well as to specify key terms of the deal and allocate key risks between buyer and seller.

The main sections of an SPA typically include *representations and warranties by the company* and the founders as to the legal and financial status of the company and its shares, the seller's right to enter into the transaction, and other important factual matters (see also Disclosure Schedules below). There is also a section where buyers of the stock make some representations and warranties back to the seller, and a section where the buyers impose *conditions which must be met* before they are obligated to buy - this section often reads like a laundry list of the other transaction documents which must be in place simultaneously. And the final section is typically a long "miscellaneous" or "other matters" section containing agreements on how the SPA will be interpreted and enforced, and documentation as to agreements on other legal matters.

## Disclosure Schedule (or Schedule of Exceptions)
The disclosure schedules are technically part of the SPA and work in concert with the section on company representation and warranties. Notwithstanding that, the disclosure schedule is worth mentioning separately because (i) it is invariably prepared as a separate parallel document alongside the SPA (and is typically not finalized until the last minute) and (ii) it contains key factual data and reference information about the company which may be useful to you later.

The way disclosure schedules typically work is that the SPA says in section x.x: "the company has no material contracts except as listed in section x.x of the disclosure schedule" or in section y.y "the company has no shares outstanding except those listed in section y.y of the disclosure schedule" or in section z.z "the company is not party to any litigation other than that listed in section z.z of the disclosure schedule."

## Investor Rights Agreement (also sometimes Registration Rights Agreement)

The IRA is where certain rights and privileges of the new stockholders are documented. The most common rights in an IRA are (i) the right to have your stock registered with the SEC as part of an IPO, so that they are freely tradable and liquid (typically after a lock-up period of 180 days or so) and note that these registration rights are sometimes handled in a separate Registration Rights Agreement (ii) the right to receive financial and management reports and information from the company and (iii) the right to participate (i.e. purchase stock in) future financings.

IRAs sometimes also contain agreements as to the establishment and composition of board and board committees and the right of the board/committees to approve corporate budgets and extra-budgetary expenditures. IRAs can spell out the stockholder's rights with respect to dividends and sometimes IRAs contain rules for calculating share price in the event of a dilutive issuance, i.e. anti-dilution protection (though this provision is more typically found in the Certificate of Incorporation) or redemption rights which are the rights to force the company to redeem your shares for cash under certain circumstances. And finally, in some IRAs you will find language about the company's obligation to pay directors expenses and indemnify directors in the event of liability in connection with board service.

## Voting Agreement

The Voting Agreement is the document used to ensure that all the signing stockholders vote in concert for the good of all. Sometimes it is just the new stockholders of one class coming in with the new round who sign the voting agreement and sometimes it is all stockholders. A voting agreement typically has provisions requiring signatories to vote to create the board structure agreed upon in the term sheet. They also typically contain what is referred to as a "drag along right" or "change of control drag along" which is the right to make the minority follow (vote for) the "will of the majority," as in approving the merger, acquisition or liquidation of the company. Often voting agreements require stockholders to vote to approve the issuance of all the new common stock necessary to convert preferred shares in the event a conversion is desirable. And typically they contain a provision stating that the stockholder automatically gives a proxy to a designate of the board to vote their shares in the event that they fail to vote them as required.

## Right of First Refusal & Co-Sale Agreement

The Right of First Refusal & Co-Sale Agreement (ROFR & CSA) is a clean-up agreement used to document a couple important rights typically included term sheets, but not appropriate for the Stock Purchase Agreement. The first of two primary things a ROFR & CSA does is to ensure that *no new shareholders are brought into the company* without first giving the company the option to buy the shares proposed to be sold (instead of the proposed third party buyer) on the same terms as the proposed buyer. ROFR & CSAs also typically state that in the event that the company does not want to buy the shares, that right goes secondarily to the existing shareholders.

The second primary thing a ROFR & CSA does is to ensure that *no existing shareholders are able to exit* their shares by selling to a third party without giving other shareholders the right to participate in that sale on the same terms and on a pro rata basis.
This may sound odd and contradictory, but think of it like both a floor and a ceiling: the effect of a ROFR & CSA is to ensure that (i) if things are going well with the company, existing shareholders, who took all the early risk, have first dibs on the company's shares and (ii) that if things are not going so great, nobody is allowed to find a buyer and get out unless everyone is allowed to participate in the partial liquidity event on a proportional basis.

The remainder of the ROFR & CSA is housekeeping to ensure that the mechanics of transfer are fair and smooth and any new shareholders are appropriately bound to the terms and conditions of the original shareholders.

## Certificate of Incorporation or Certificate of Amendment (Articles of Incorporation in California)

It may seem odd to include a copy of state filing in a deal like this, but the reason this document is included in most early stage equity financings is fairly clever and sensible. Here's why: for most early stage financings, a new class of preferred stock is created, and the preferences or privileges of that class of stock is recorded in the company's Certificate or Articles of Incorporation. These key rights typically include liquidation preferences (getting paid before common stock or other classes of stock), dilution protection in the event of a down round, voting rights, election of directors, dividend rights, and rights relating to conversion into common stock.

What is sensible about that? Two things: (1) State law generally requires the affirmative vote of approval by the holders of a class of shares for a negative change to any of the rights of those shares, so preferred shareholders are going to have legal protection and the right to vote on any changes to their rights and privileges. For example, Delaware law says that the holders of a class must vote to approve any change which: "Increases or decreases the aggregate number of authorized shares of the affected class(es); or Adversely affects the powers, preferences, or special rights of the shares of such class." (2) Because company Certificates of Incorporation are public state filings, anyone considering purchasing the stock of a company has the right to inspect the special privileges given out to the shareholders of preferred stock and know that they are getting themselves into.

## Legal Opinion

Investors buying stock in a company generally require counsel for the company to stake their reputation "vouching" for the legal status of the company and the validity of the transaction. Legal opinions in this context generally start with a recitation of all of the items counsel has reviewed prior to giving the opinion (deal documents, corporate records) and then go on to say, with varying degrees of wiggle room reserved, (i) that the company is validly existing and in good standing in the state in which it is formed, (ii) that the signing of the transaction documents is legal and accompanied by the necessary approvals and consents, (iii) exactly what the outstanding capitalization of the company is, (iv) that the issuance of the stock is legal under the relevant SEC exemptions, and (v) that there is no material litigation pending. Some things may be added and some of the wording may vary, but these are the basic things investors look for in a legal opinion.

## Accredited Investor Questionnaire/Certification

The vast majority of early stage equity financings are done pursuant to an exemption from the registration and disclosure requirements normally imposed by the US Securities and Exchange Commission on the sale of securities to the public. The scope of the exemption is rather narrow, and among other things, it requires that shares in exempt deals be sold only to accredited investors who are presumed to be sophisticated enough to evaluate a deal without public disclosure and wealthy enough to withstand a total loss stemming from an exempt deal. The accredited investor questionnaire is the document which investors fill out and sign to certify that they are accredited investors eligible to participate in an exempt offering. This questionnaire is not always a separate document - its concepts and certification are sometimes incorporated in the Stock Purchase Agreement or other deal document instead.

## Signature Pages

Technically these are not a separate document in any sense of the word - typically this term merely refers to a separate electronic or paper *file* containing all the signature pages of all the deal documents collected together in one single document for the convenience of a signing party. Once signed, they are attached on your behalf to the relevant documents, counter-signed by the company and returned to you as part of the final closing documents package or "closing binder." Sometimes when looking for key numerical information about your shareholdings or other tracking information for your Seraf account, you can find key bits right next to your signature in the signature pages.

# Occasionally Used Deal Documents in Stock Transactions

This section covers documents which turn up from time to time. It is not a problem or concern if they are not used in a given deal; it may just mean: (i) the issues to which they relate are covered in other agreements (ii) the issues to which they relate are not present or relevant in this particular deal or (iii) the lawyers drafting the deal documents have a different drafting style.

## Capitalization Table

Early stage equity financings will often, but not always, include a detailed chart or table laying out all of the ownership positions of the different stockholders of the company including common stockholders, preferred stockholders and option and warrant holders (technically these last two are security holders not stockholders.) The capitalization table may either document the various positions *before the close* of the new round, *after the close*, or preferably both in one document. Often the Capitalization Table, or at least a high level summary of it, will be included in the Disclosure Schedule (above), but sometimes it is distributed as a stand-alone document. Capitalization tables often prove useful down the road (for example, when trying to double-check proper payouts in an exit), so it is not a bad idea to ask for a copy of the current cap table every time you invest in a company or sign deal documents. Then just upload them to Seraf with the round and you will always have them for reference.

## Board Consent

A company must generally have the approval of its board to be authorized to partake in an equity financing. This approval is typically recorded in board minutes of a live meeting but sometimes permission is sought and recorded in writing by means of a unanimous written consent; in those cases, a copy of that written consent is sometimes included in the deal document package.

## Stockholder Consent & Waiver

Similar to the board consent, under the Certificate of Incorporation or bylaws of a company an equity financing can require shareholder approval as well as board approval, so a stockholder consent is often included in as part of the deal. Sometimes it is part of one of the principal deal documents, and sometimes it is a stand-alone document. If the rights of shareholders are being changed or cut back by the terms of the new deal, an explicit waiver of the abridged rights may be included to make it abundantly clear that everyone is onboard with the deal.

## Irrevocable Proxy

In a typical equity deal, voting matters are left to the individual shareholders. The assumption is that it is relatively easy for a major investor to put together a majority block in favor of a proposal the major investor would like to see passed. Or a voting agreement is used. But in some deals, nothing is left to chance and investors are asked to assign their voting rights to an investor delegate (this assignment is called giving a proxy to a proxy holder) who can then vote the rights. This is a way of ensuring that shares get voted, blocks get neatly formed and no one has to spend effort or incur delay chasing votes for desirable outcomes. These proxy assignments are generally permanent and irreversible (hence the name irrevocable) transfers of voting rights, so if you see one in a deal package, read it carefully and make sure you are comfortable that the proxy holder's interests fully align with yours.

## Indemnification Agreement

Although companies generally carry Directors' and Officers' insurance to protect directors from the damages and expenses of shareholder lawsuits alleging that they did something wrong as a director, many highly skilled and sought-after directors want additional protection if they are going to be convinced to serve. What companies do in that situation is offer to, in effect, re-insure the directors by indemnifying them (agreeing to reimburse them or "hold them harmless") for any expenses or damages they incur while doing their job competently and in good faith. The way this is recorded is in an indemnification clause in one of the principal deal documents, or as a stand-alone indemnification agreement. They are long and jargon-laden documents, but what they basically say is that if the director is doing a good job and acting in good faith, and they get sued by shareholders, the company will make them whole. There are a lot of details about the precise conditions in which such reimbursement will occur and the limits on that reimbursement, but if you see one of these, the concept is pretty simple - the company will cover the directors' costs.

## Secretary's Certificate

The Secretary's Certificate is essentially a small cover sheet attesting to the authenticity and accuracy of the copies of the various deal approvals and governance documents. They are typically worded as a series of paragraphs each starting out with "attached is a true and correct copy of the…" and going on to list the bylaws, the board and stockholder resolutions approving the transaction, the names and titles of the current list of officers of the company and the certificates of good standing and legal existence from the state of incorporation. And they are signed by the secretary of the corporation (who often is the CEO in small companies.)

## Compliance Certificate

The compliance certificate is a belt-and-suspenders document intended to give investors extra protection by requiring the company's CEO to personally take responsibility for the transaction.

Compliance certificates typically include statements that (i) all the representations and warranties the company has made in the deal documents are true, (ii) that the company has obtained all the consents, approvals, permits and waivers it needed to obtain, (iii) the shares being issued are duly authorized, and (iv) newly revised Certificate of Incorporation has been filed and is in effect. And they conclude with a simple signature from the CEO.

## Joinder Agreement

Joinder agreements are sometimes used as an easy way to make new investors a party to existing agreements - they literally join you in with the other signatories. They typically list the specific agreements and their dates and make it clear that by signing the joinder agreement, the new investor is signing, and means to be bound by, all the other agreements listed.

## Founder Stock Agreement (aka Vesting Agreement or Restricted Share Agreement)

Term sheets in early-stage equity deals often require that the founders stock be subject to forfeit in the event they leave the company. This concept is sometimes inaccurately nicknamed "founder vesting" but in fact what going on is that founders are agreeing to put a layer of contractual claw-back on top of stock they already own. Given this, "restrictions lapsing" is technically more correct language than "stock vesting," but the economics are equivalent. The claw-backs amount to an agreement that they will forfeit the stock (at a typically very low price so as to not cause a cash crunch for the company) if they leave. The vesting nickname stems from the fact that these restrictions lapse as time goes by. These arrangements are usually documented in agreements variously named things like Founder Stock Agreement or Vesting Agreement or Restricted Share Agreement. Investors are typically not a party to these, but a copy is sometimes furnished to them as proof of their existence because of the importance of the issue.

## Risk Factors Statement

A list of risk factors is sometimes furnished to the investors as a way of limiting various types of liability for the company in the event that things do not go as planned or shareholders become unhappy. They literally serve as a "can't say we didn't warn you" device and work by disclosing a variety of risks associated with the investment. Example risks you might see include: the stock being offered is not registered and not liquid, the terms of your deal might be renegotiated in a later financing, the company has a limited operating history and may not be successful, the company has limited operating capital and might run out of money and either fail or need to raise more money on less attractive terms, competitors may out-compete the company, customers may not like the product, the company may not get sufficient intellectual property protection, the company may not be able to attract and retain enough good talent, etc. At most you will be required to acknowledge that you got your copy.

## A Guide to Angel Investing Docs - Convertible Debt Deal

Compared to stock deals, there are a smaller number of types of deal documents used in convertible debt transactions. For the purposes of clarity, we've divided them into Commonly Used and Occasionally Used. Readers should also keep in mind that this article talks in generalities in terms of where concepts are typically covered - every deal is different and a given issue may be addressed in a different document in your deal.

# Commonly Used Deal Documents in Convertible Debt Deals

## Promissory Note

The Promissory Note (or Convertible Promissory Note) is the actual debt instrument in the deal. In reality it is nothing more than a fancy I.O.U. It states the name of the borrower, the date of the debt, the amount of indebtedness, the interest rate, the interest rate calculation mechanism (annual, semi-annual, cumulative, non-cumulative) and the maturity date (due date). Then usually immediately after those terms there will be some discussion of any negotiated cap on the conversion price or discount against the conversion price if the deal features a cap or discount.

The rest of the note is typically dedicated to setting out the mechanics of converting the debt repayment into stock. In this section you will find language outlining what constitutes a qualified financing - a note-holder does not want stock in a company that is underfunded (she would rather have a cash repayment), so the concept here is to say that it needs to be part of a pretty robust financing if you are going to convert me into stock. There is also typically some language about what happens if there is no qualified financing before the maturity date. And the final few paragraphs are the usual legal housekeeping clauses about contractual interpretation and enforcement.

*Special Terms: Subordination, Security Interests and Guarantees* - Occasionally notes will incorporate the concept of subordination, security interests or guarantees. These features are more typical of classic bank type debt, and less common in investor convertible debt, but they are worth mentioning because they do show up occasionally.

- *Subordination* is a legal concept where a lender agrees that its right to receive repayment is subordinate to (i.e. in a lower position or in second priority to) another lender's right to repayment. For example, most banks who have lent to a company will immediately recall their loan if the company tries to borrow from investors unless investors agree their debt is subordinate to the bank's debt.
- *Security Interests* are legal rights allowing the lender to more easily seize collateral in the event of a default on the loan. A note that includes a security interest is called a secured note. These security interests require additional state filings to perfect and they are typically signaled in the title of the instrument (e.g. Convertible Secured Note) or right near the beginning of the text.
- *Guarantees* are personal undertakings by someone involved in a corporation to repay the corporation's debt if the corporation fails or defaults on the debt. Banks typically insist on personal guarantees from CEOs before lending, and they may take a security interest in the CEO's home or some other major asset as collateral. Personal guarantees are not common with straight investor debt and probably best avoided - either you believe enough in the CEO and the concept to invest and assume the risk of failure, or you don't.

# Occasionally Used Deal Documents in Convertible Debt Deals

## Note Purchase Agreement
A Note Purchase Agreement (sometimes called a Subscription Agreement - see below) is a contractual wrapper that makes a note financing a little bit more formal and a little bit more like a stock financing. It typically outlines the mechanics of the closing (to make sure no individual note holders get caught out as the only ones investing), it adds in some representations and warranties on the part of the company around validity and authorization, it add some note holders reps and warranties around eligibility as an accredited investor, and in some rare cases, it may serve to cover some of the key provisions you might expect to see in a Note Holders Agreement or a Voting Agreement (both discussed below.)

## Subscription Agreement
A note Subscription Agreement is very similar to a Note Purchase Agreement (above) - mostly it is just a naming convention. Occasionally, however, you will see subscription agreements used to take some of the more complex terms of a note out of the note itself and into a separate subscription contract such that the note and the subscription agreement work as two halves of one convertible debt deal. The effect of doing it this way is the same, it just allows for a more simple note and a more thorough treatment of conversion mechanics in a more traditional contract format.

## Note Holders Agreements and Voting Agreements
Sometimes the holders of a note will insist on things like board seats, information rights, covenants against issuing stock or other debt and/or other terms more typically associated with stock deals. When this happens these contractual agreements between the company and the note holders are usually written up in a separate agreement given a title like Note Holders' Agreement or Voting Agreement.

## Subordination Agreement
Sometimes subordination of debt (see above) is done in a stand-alone agreement. This most often occurs when new debt is added after the debt to be subordinated is already in place - for example when there is an outstanding convertible debt round and a revolving line of credit from a bank is added, and the parties enter into a new agreement to make it clear that the old debt is subordinate to the new debt.

## Warrant to Purchase Stock

One of the complaints about convertible notes in the early stage context is that they amount to equity risk for debt returns. People try to address this with the terms of the note - for example caps on the conversion price and discounts on the conversion price. But these mechanisms do not fully align the interests of the founders and the note holders, so in an effort to better address that, sometimes warrants to purchase shares are given in lieu of or in addition to caps and discounts. It obviously makes the note perform economically more like equity since warrants literally are equity, but warrants do introduce a bit of complexity into what is supposed to be a simple transaction.

## Sample Termsheet - Preferred Stock

This short simple example termsheet is intended to give readers a sense of what a very basic termsheet looks like. This particular example is called the Series Seed Termsheet v. 3.2 and is the work and property of the Series Seed project (www.seriesseed.com).  Please review their SeriesSeed.com site for important information and disclaimers regarding use of this term sheet and its accompanying documents.

Sharp eyed readers will note that this highly simplified termsheet does not address some of the important issues discussed in this Termsheet course such as anti-dilution, certain approval rights, ROFR and Co-Sale rights, or drag-along rights. It is intended for the smallest and simplest priced rounds and we selected it for that simplicity to give a sense of what a basic termsheet looks like. If you wish to add some of those clauses back in, please refer to the example language in the speaker notes in the instructor version of this material.

# TERMS FOR PRIVATE PLACEMENT OF SERIES SEED PREFERRED STOCK OF
[*Insert Company Name*], INC.
### [Date]

The following is a summary of the principal terms with respect to the proposed Series Seed Preferred Stock financing of [_____], Inc., a [Delaware] corporation (the "***Company***"). Except for the section entitled "Binding Terms," this summary of terms does not constitute a legally binding obligation. The parties intend to enter into a legally binding obligation only pursuant to definitive agreements to be negotiated and executed by the parties.

## **Offering Terms**

| | |
|---|---|
| Securities to Issue: | Shares of Series Seed Preferred Stock of the Company (the "***Series Seed***"). |
| Aggregate Proceeds: | $[_____] in aggregate. |
| Purchasers: | [Accredited investors approved by the Company] (the "***Purchasers***"). |
| Price Per Share: | Price per share (the "***Original Issue Price***"), based on a pre-money valuation of $[____], including an available option pool of [____]%. |
| Liquidation Preference: | One times the Original Issue Price plus declared but unpaid dividends on each share of Series Seed, balance of proceeds paid to Common. A merger, reorganization or similar transaction will be treated as a liquidation. |
| Conversion: | Convertible into one share of Common (subject to proportional adjustments for stock splits, stock dividends and the like) at any time at the option of the holder. |
| Voting Rights: | Votes together with the Common Stock on all matters on an asconverted basis. Approval of a majority of the Preferred Stock required to (i) adversely change rights of the Preferred Stock; (ii) change the authorized number of shares; (iii) authorize a new series of Preferred Stock having rights senior to or on parity with the Preferred Stock; (iv) redeem or repurchase any shares (other than pursuant to employee or consultant agreements); (v) declare or pay any dividend; (vi) change the number of directors; or (vii) liquidate or dissolve, including any change of control. |
| Documentation: | Documents will be identical to the Series Seed Preferred Stock documents published at www.seriesseed.com, except for the modifications set forth in this Term Sheet. |
| Financial Information: | Purchasers who have invested at least [$_____] ("***Major Purchasers***") will receive standard information and inspection rights and management rights letter. |
| Participation Right: | Major Purchasers will have the right to participate on a pro rata basis in subsequent issuances of equity securities. |
| Board of Directors: | [____] directors elected by holders of a majority of common stock, [____] elected by holders of a majority of Series Seed and [____] elected by mutual consent. |
| Expenses: | Company to reimburse counsel to Purchasers for a flat fee of $10,000. |
| Future Rights: | The Series Seed will be given the same rights as the next series of Preferred Stock (with appropriate adjustments for economic terms). |
| Key Holder Matters | Each Key Holder shall have four years vesting beginning [_____]. Full acceleration upon "Double Trigger." Each Key Holder shall have assigned all relevant IP to the Company before closing. |

Binding Terms:   For a period of thirty days, the Company shall not solicit offers from other parties for any financing. Without the consent of Purchasers, the Company shall not disclose these terms to anyone other than officers, directors, key service providers, and other potential Purchasers in this financing.

COMPANY: [_____, INC.]

PURCHASERS:

_____

_____

Name: _____

Name: _____

Title: _____

Title: _____

Date: _____

Date: _____

## Sample Termsheet - Convertible Note

This simple convertible note termsheet is intended to give readers a sense of what a very basic set of convertible note deal terms looks like. Readers should be advised that this particular example includes reference to a supplemental noteholders' agreement which is a separate contract to specify additional rights and obligations not included in a typical form of convertible note. These additional rights would include things ranging from basic corporate representations, to basic governance, to investor relations and financial information reporting. Supplemental Noteholders' Agreements are not required or even necessarily standard in convertible note deals, but they are strongly recommended as a good mitigation for some of the key limitations of using the convertible note deal structure.

_____, INC.

## SUMMARY OF PROPOSED TERMS FOR
## CONVERTIBLE PROMISSORY NOTE FINANCING

The following is a summary of the basic terms and conditions of a proposed convertible promissory note financing of _____, Inc., a [Delaware] / [Massachusetts] / [_____] corporation (the "*Company*"). This term sheet is for discussion purposes only and is not binding on Company or the Investors (as defined below), nor is Company or any of the Investors obligated to consummate the convertible promissory note financing until a definitive convertible note purchase agreement has been agreed to and executed by Company and the Investors.

| | |
|---|---|
| *Financing Amount:* | Up to $_____ in aggregate principal amount of convertible promissory notes (the "*Notes*"). |
| *Closings:* | The Company may close the sale of the Notes in one or more closings with one or more purchasers of the Notes acceptable to the Company. |
| *Note Purchase Agreement:* | The Notes will be issued and sold pursuant to a convertible note purchase agreement acceptable to the Company's legal counsel and will contain representations and warranties of the Company and the Investors (the "*Note Purchase Agreement*") as sumarized below.<br><br>Company Representations & Covenants:<br>• Organization, good standing, power and authorization<br>• Corporate use of proceeds<br>• Capitalization<br>• Employee agreements<br>• Investor reporting<br>Investor Representations:<br>• Information, accreditation, sophistication and ability to bear risk<br>• Obligation to hold |
| *Maturity Date:* | Principal and unpaid accrued interest on the Notes will be due and payable in 24 months (the "*Maturity Date*"). |

| | |
|---|---|
| *Interest:* | Simple interest will accrue on an annual basis at the rate of 6% per annum based on a 365 day year. |
| *Conversion to Equity:* | Automatic Conversion in a Qualified Financing. If the Company issues equity securities ("***Equity Securities***") in a transaction or series of related transactions resulting in aggregate gross new proceeds to the Company of at least $500,000 not including conversion of the Notes and any other indebtedness (a "***Qualified Financing***"), then the Notes, and any accrued but unpaid interest thereon, will automatically convert into the equity securities issued pursuant to the Qualified Financing at a conversion price equal to the lesser of (i) 80% of the per share price paid by the purchasers of such equity securities in the Qualified Financing or (ii) the price equal to the quotient of [*valuation cap on note*] $_____ divided by the aggregate number of outstanding shares of the Company's Common Stock as of immediately prior to the initial closing of the Qualified Financing (assuming full conversion or exercise of all convertible or exercisable securities then outstanding other than the Notes) (the "***Capped Conversion Price***").<br><br>Voluntary Conversion at the Maturity Date. If the Notes have not been previously converted pursuant to a Qualified Financing, then, following the Maturity Date, the Requisite Holders (as defined below) may elect to convert all of the Notes into shares of the Company's Common Stock at a conversion price equal to the Capped Conversion Price. |
| *Sale of the Company:* | If a Qualified Financing has not occurred and the Company elects to consummate a sale of the Company prior to the Maturity Date, then notwithstanding any provision of the Notes to the contrary, the holders of the Notes will receive the greater of (i) an amount that they would have received had the Notes converted into Common Stock at the Capped Conversion Price, or (ii) the Company will pay the holder of each Note an aggregate amount equal to 1.5 times the aggregate amount of principal and interest then outstanding under such Note in full satisfaction of the Company's obligations under such Note. |

| | |
|---|---|
| *Pre-Payment:* | The principal and accrued interest may not be prepaid unless approved in writing by Investors holding Notes whose aggregate principal amount represents a majority of the outstanding principal amount of all then-outstanding Notes (the "**Requisite Holders**"). |
| *Financial Information:* | Holders of the Notes will receive quarterly and annual financial information. |
| *Capital Structure:* | The Company's capitalization prior to the Closing shall include an option pool of 15%. The capitalization of the Company as of the date hereof is attached to this Term Sheet. |
| *Amendment and Waiver:* | The Note Purchase Agreement and the Notes may be amended, or any term thereof waived, upon the written consent of the Company and the Requisite Holders. |
| *Board of Directors:* | As soon as feasible after the Closing, the company shall establish a Board of Directors. The Board of Directors shall be set at three members and shall initially consist of: A [CEO], B, as the investor representative (the "Investor Designee") and C an independent person acceptable to the other two board members. |
| *No Security Interest:* | The Notes will be a general unsecured obligation of the Company. |
| *Non-Disclosure/Assignment of Invention Agreement:* | Prior to the initial closing, each founder, employee, officer and consultant of the Company will have entered into a customary Non-Disclosure and Assignment of Inventions Agreement. |
| *Fees and Expenses:* | Each Investor will bear its own fees and expenses incurred in the transactions contemplated by this term sheet. |

Issued By:                                         Accepted: _____, Inc

__[SAMPLE – NOT FOR SIGNATURE]__       By: __[SAMPLE]_____


Date: _____          Date: _____

## Valuation Modeling Tool

This valuation modeling tool is designed to help investors determine a reasonable valuation for a potential investment based on market conditions for:

1. Exit Realities
2. Financing Requirements
3. Current Deal Environment

# Exit Realities

The purpose of Worksheet One is to ballpark the kind of exit that might be possible and use that to create the first set of adjustments to the starting valuation. With Worksheet One you will walk through a series of simple questions to help you make "Exit Realities" adjustments to your valuation. When you boil all the relevant concepts down, here is how it looks. For each topic you want to "set the slider" in the right place and tally up your resulting Worksheet One sub-total to be carried forward:

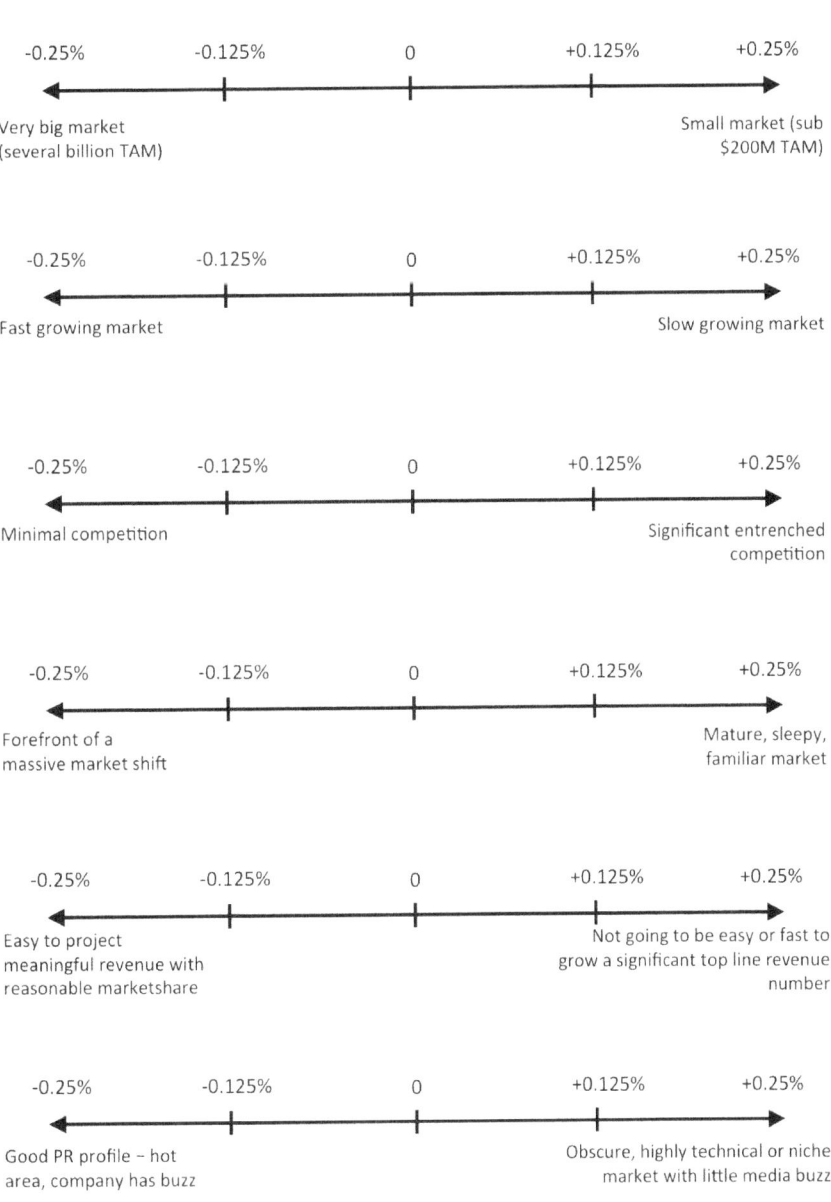

## Valuation Worksheet One: Exit Realities (cont.)

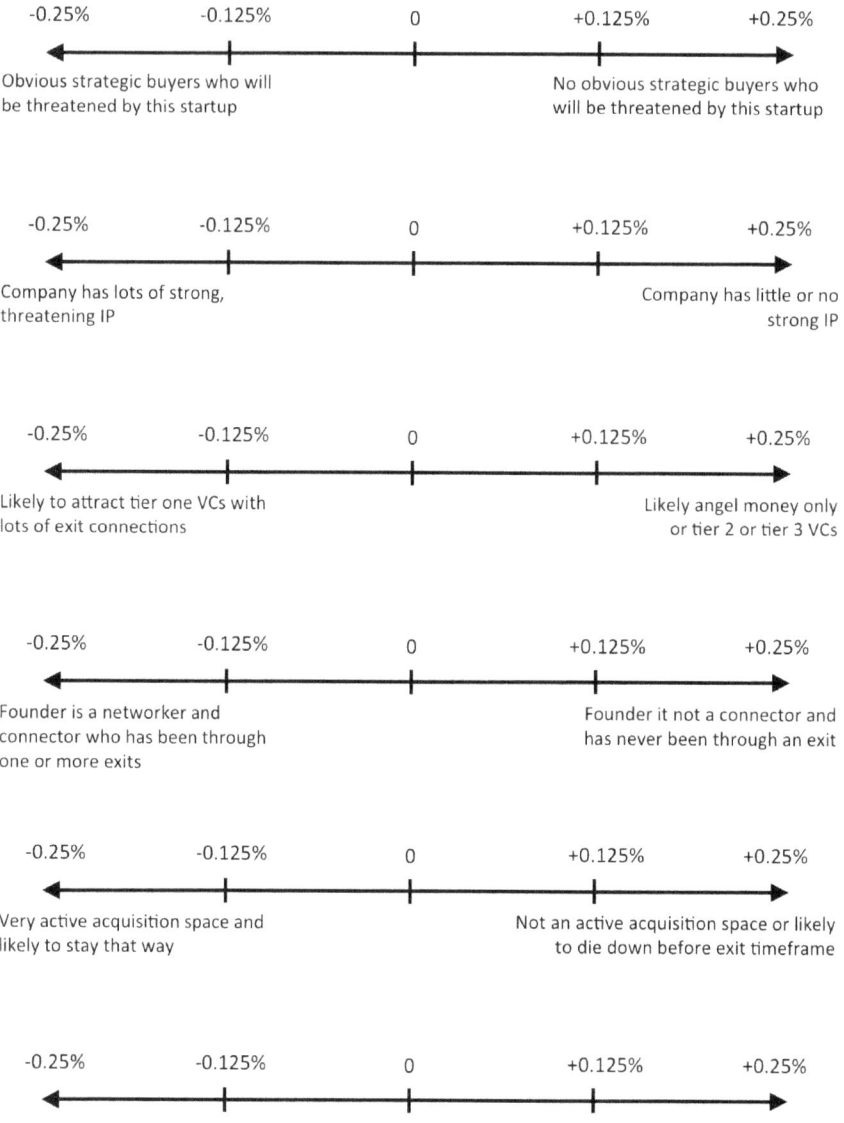

# Financing Requirements

The purpose of Worksheet Two is to gauge how much capital it is going to take to move the company to the most logical point of exit and estimate the impact that financing plan should have on the valuation you should pay. This is important to assess in the valuation context because, more capital required means more financing risk and more dilution for you, both of which drastically affect your returns. Capital **should** also enable more growth, but it **definitely does** mean more financing risk and dilution. Again, for each topic you want to "set the slider" in the right place and tally up your resulting Worksheet Two sub-total to be carried forward. When you boil all the relevant concepts down, here is how it looks.

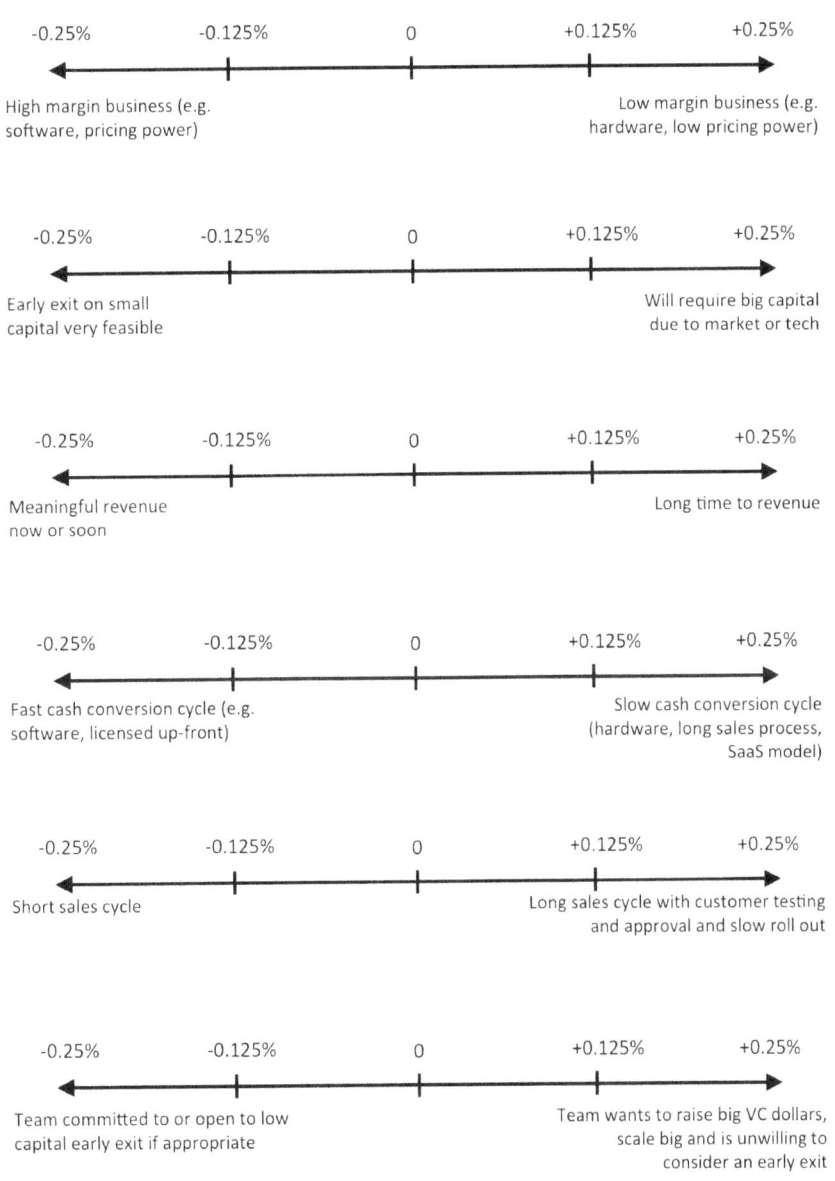

Valuation Worksheet Two: Financing Requirements

## Valuation Worksheet Two: Financing Requirements (cont.)

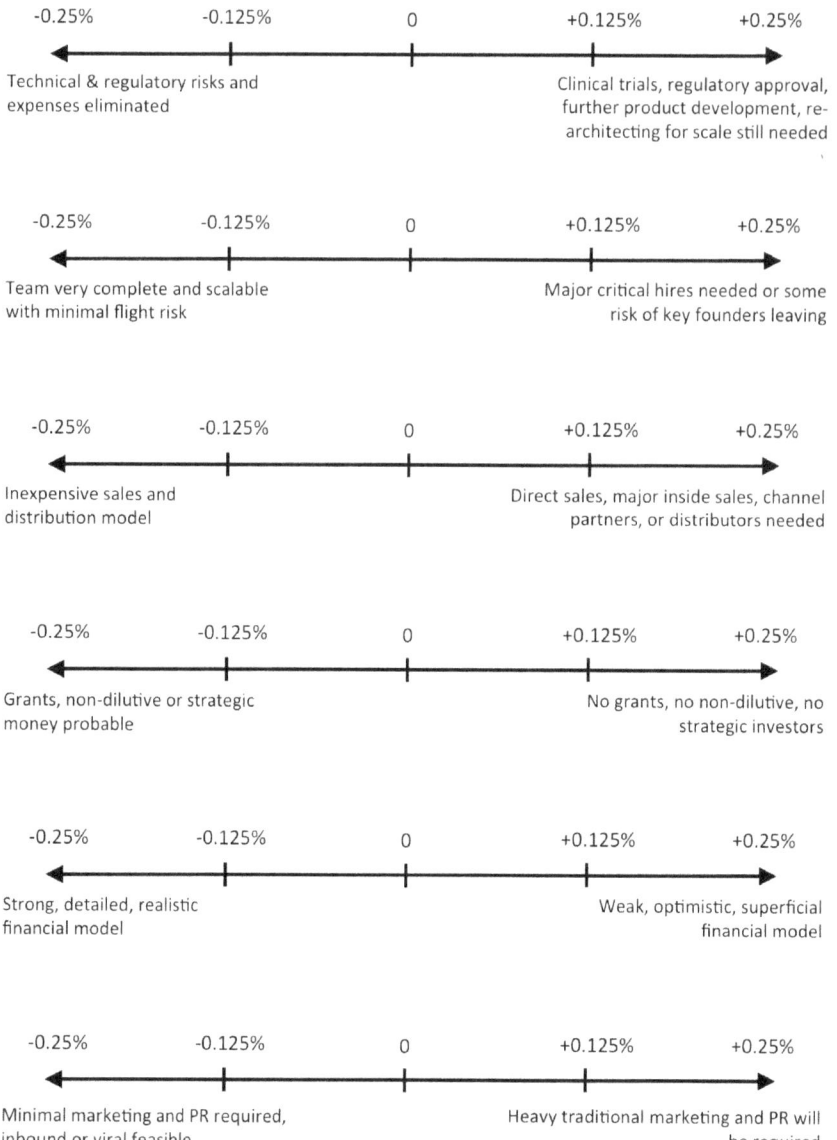

# Current Deal Environment

Worksheet Three helps you assess the relative attractiveness of a particular deal in the real world market context of your market at the relevant moment in time. How many times have you heard someone explain away a deal that couldn't raise money, or a deal that raised at a seemingly crazy high valuation as "a function of the market" or "what the market will bear"? Investors may like to think we have valuation completely down to a science, but the reality is that market conditions and the relative attractiveness of a company affect the valuation tremendously. Below is what Worksheet Three looks like. As with the other two, you need to set the sliders to reflect how the deal scores on the key issues and carry that subtotal forward.

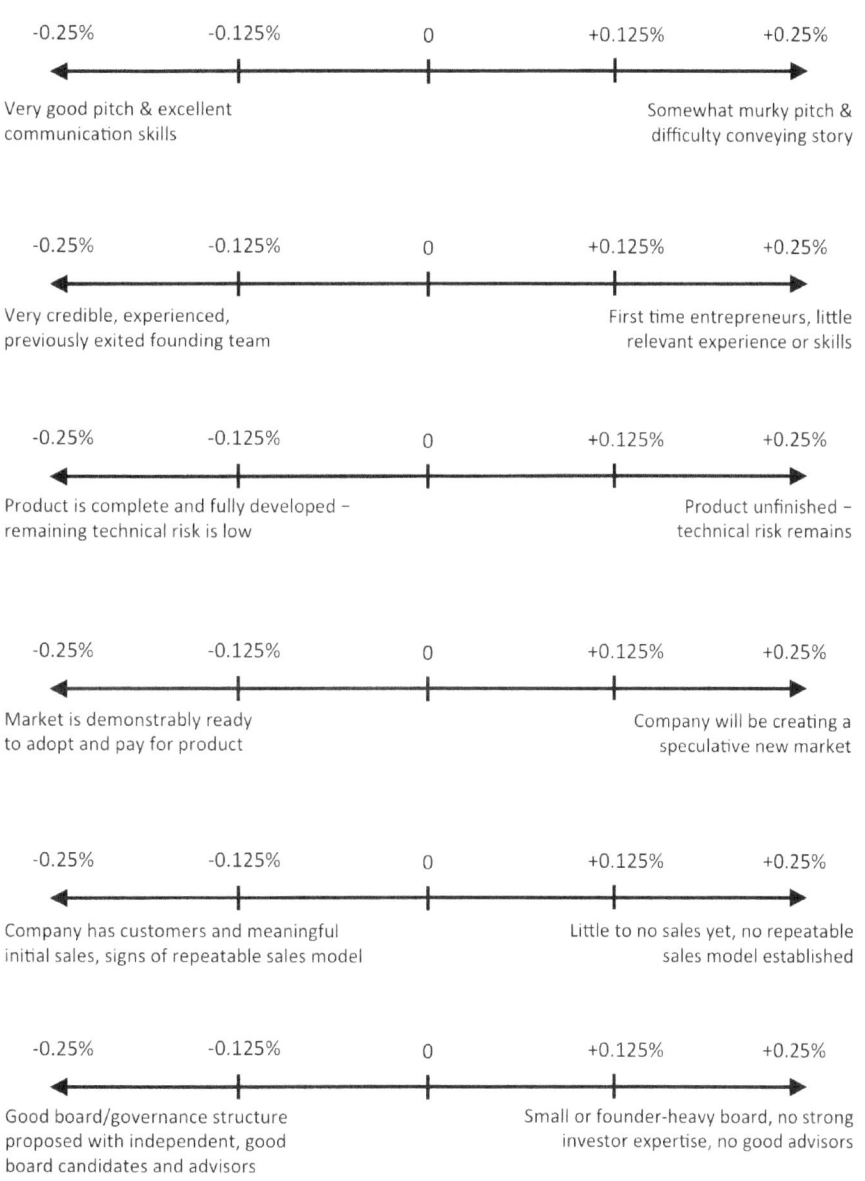

Valuation Worksheet Three: Current Deal & Environment

# Valuation Worksheet Three: Current Deal & Environment (cont.)

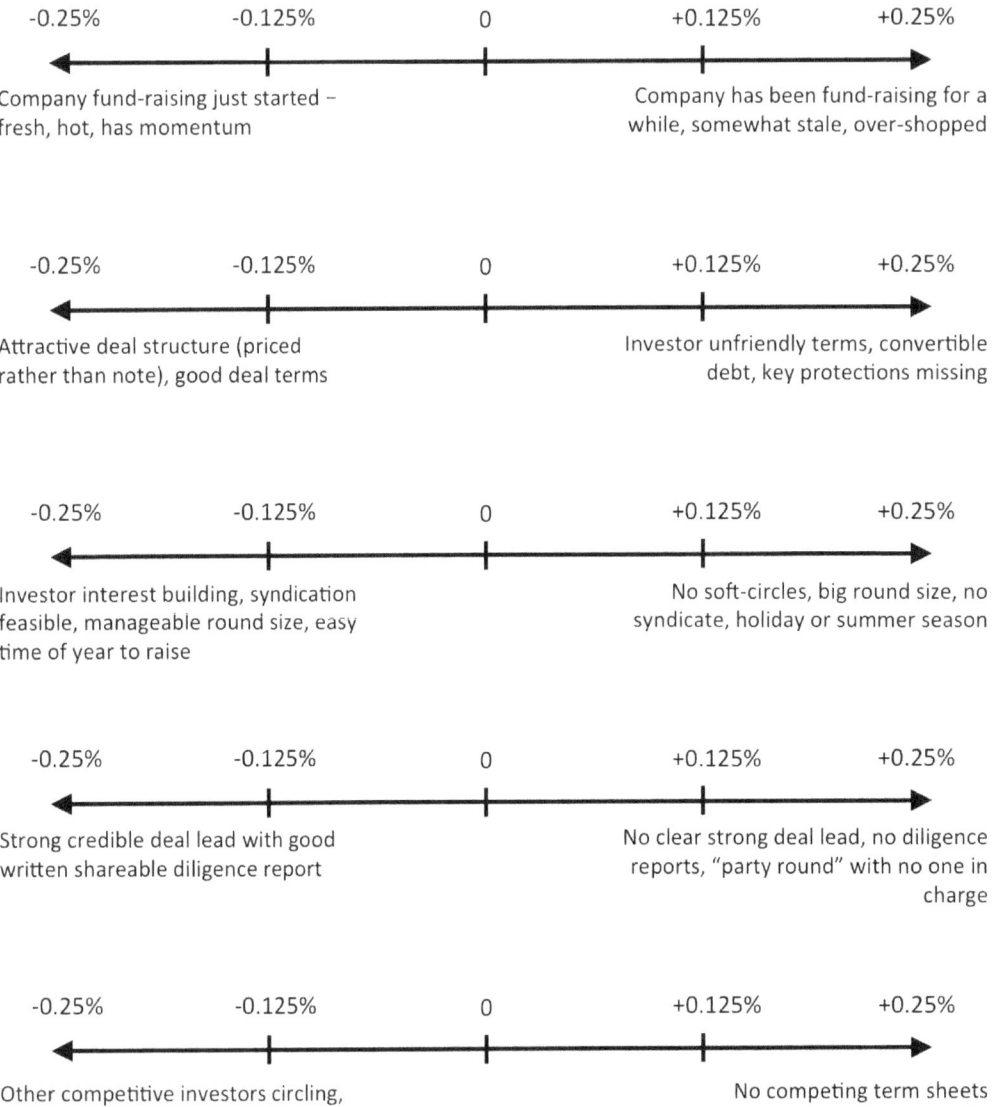

# Valuation Lookup Table

For the final step of the Seraf Method for valuing early stage companies, we bring it all together and apply our adjustments to a valuation starting point. As the Berkus, Payne and Risk Factor Methods illustrate, you have to start somewhere. But, in our view, an approach based on picking an arbitrary one-size-fits-all number does not drive a good enough result. To find a reasonable starting point, you have to take into account historical market norms and the size of your particular deal. Market statistics can help with that. Thinking of it in terms of percentage ownership is a good yardstick. In our experience, different size rounds tend to be associated with different ownership percentages. To utilize the Valuation Look-Up Table and obtain your final valuation adjustment, the spreadsheet carries forward your net adjustment from the first three worksheets and applies them to the Valuation Look-Up Table. For example, if you found a company that looked really good, the first three worksheets might net out to an adjustment downward of half a percentage point in the amount investors feel they need to own, with a resulting increase in the valuation investors are willing to pay.

| | |
|---|---|
| Adjustment Carried From Worksheet One | -0.250 |
| Adjustment Carried From Worksheet Two | -0.250 |
| Adjustment Carried From Worksheet Three | -0.375 |
| **Total Worksheet Four Adjustment** | **-0.00875** [Note: divided by 100 to make a percentage for calculation purposes] |

| ROUND SIZE | BASE PERCENT TO BE OWNED | ADJUSTED PERCENT OWNED | PRE- MONEY VALUATION | POST- MONEY VALUATION |
|---|---|---|---|---|
| $500,000 | 25.00% | 24.13% | $1,572,539 | $2,072,539 |
| $600,000 | 24.75% | 23.88% | $1,913,089 | $2,513,089 |
| $700,000 | 24.50% | 23.63% | $2,262,963 | $2,962,963 |
| $800,000 | 24.25% | 23.38% | $2,622,460 | $3,422,460 |
| $900,000 | 24.00% | 23.13% | $2,991,892 | $3,891,892 |
| $1,000,000 | 23.75% | 22.88% | $3,371,585 | $4,371,585 |
| $1,100,000 | 23.50% | 22.63% | $3,761,878 | $4,861,878 |

## Capitalization Tables with Waterfall Analysis

Have you ever been in a situation where you are negotiating an investment with an entrepreneur and you can't agree on the pre-money valuation? Any early stage investor who makes more than one or two investments will certainly run into this issue. It's never an easy discussion, so it helps if you are prepared ahead of time with concrete facts and figures for your recommended valuation. If you do a little homework, not only might you be surprised how little difference small changes in valuation make for founders, you will also be armed to have a very educational discussion with the entrepreneurs.

Let's play out a scenario that Christopher and I ran into recently with a company in which we were looking to invest. At a high level, here are the key facts about the company today, along with a few assumptions we will make about the future of the company.

- The company is pre-revenue and needs to raise $1.25M to get their product shipping and close their first few customer deals.
- We were willing to invest at a $3.6M pre-money valuation. The entrepreneur insisted on a $4M valuation.
- We assumed the company will need an additional $5M Series B financing to get all the way to an exit.
- We assumed the Series B round will be priced at 2X the post-money valuation of the Series A round, and both rounds will be Non-Participating Preferred.
- We assumed that approximately 5% of the common shares are held by employees, directors and advisors.
- We assumed an exit for the company will be somewhere in the $25M to $100M range.

So, given those facts and assumptions, what difference does our requested valuation ($3.6M) versus the entrepreneur's desired valuation ($4M) actually make to the returns of each party?

|  | $3.6M Series A Valuation | $4M Series A Valuation |
| --- | --- | --- |
| **$25M Exit** |  |  |
| Founders | $9.3M | $9.9M |
| Series A Shareholders | $4.6M | $4.3M |
| **$50M Exit** |  |  |
| Founders | $18.7M | $19.7M |
| Series A Shareholders | $9.1M | $8.7M |
| **$100M Exit** |  |  |
| Founders | $37.3M | $39.5M |
| Series A Shareholders | $18.2M | $17.3M |

Note that our $3.6M pre-money offer is 10% less than the founder's $4M pre-money expectation. The final outcome for the entrepreneur in all of the above exit scenarios shows about a 5% to 6% difference in what they will ultimately receive upon an exit. Even though it feels to the entrepreneur that our respective valuations are miles apart, the reality is about half the difference in the end.

It is probably worth pointing out to the entrepreneur that there are two further advantages for them in keeping the pre-money reasonable:

It makes it easier to bring investors into the round so that they can finish the fund-raising quickly and get back to focusing on the operations of the company. And, it means the post-money valuation will be more reasonable, which means it will be less of a yoke around their necks (see Chapter 2) as they head into the uncertainties that lie ahead and try to grow into justifying their valuation for the next round.

So hopefully you are convinced it is worth doing some modeling. But how can you easily do this type of financial modeling to help better understand valuation and exit scenarios? You need a good Cap Table and Waterfall Analysis tool.

If you perform a Google search for the term "Cap Table", you will end up with dozens of options to choose from. These options include everything from Excel spreadsheets that build simple cap tables all the way along the spectrum to complex, high-end software products that will track everything you need for a complete cap table. But we built one we think you might prefer using.

So why did we bother creating another cap table tool when there are so many options out there? We did it for several reasons:

1. We wanted a tool that was very simple to set up. We didn't want to have to enter lots of data to model a cap table.
2. We wanted a tool that allowed us to model a variety of different exit scenarios to help understand how much each shareholder would get depending on the size of the exit.
3. We wanted a tool that was free for everyone to use with no strings attached.

We chose the familiar Google Sheets platform and created two separate documents. The first sheet allows you to create a cap table with just a single Series A round of financing for very basic modeling.

### Valuations, Investments and Share Price

|  | Series A |
|---|---|
| Pre-Money Valuation | $3,175,000 |
| Total Invested in Round | $1,250,000 |
| Post-Money Valuation | $4,425,000 |
| Price / Share | $1.25 |
| Liquidation Preference | 1 |
| Participating Preferred | Yes |

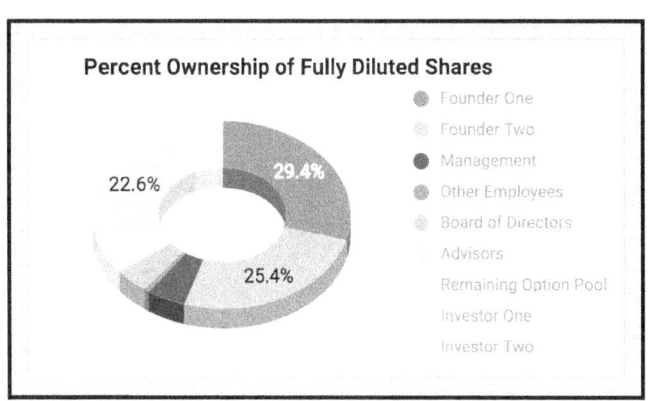

| Shareholders | Common Shares | Options | Series A Preferred Shares | Series A Investment | Total Share Ownership | Percentage of Fully Diluted Shares |
|---|---|---|---|---|---|---|
| **Shares and Options owned by the Founders of the Company** | | | | | | |
| Founder One | 1,000,000 |  | 40,000 | $50,000 | 1,040,000 | **29.4%** |
| Founder Two | 900,000 |  |  |  | 900,000 | **25.4%** |
| **Shares and Options owned by Employees, Advisors & Directors** | | | | | | |
| Management | 100,000 | 75,000 |  |  | 175,000 | **4.9%** |
| Other Employees |  | 25,000 |  |  | 25,000 | **0.7%** |
| Board of Directors |  | 30,000 | 120,000 | $150,000 | 150,000 | **4.2%** |
| Advisors |  | 10,000 |  |  | 10,000 | **0.3%** |
| Remaining Option Pool |  | 200,000 |  |  | 200,000 | **5.6%** |
| **Shares Acquired by Investors** | | | | | | |
| Investor One | 200,000 |  | 600,000 | $750,000 | 800,000 | **22.6%** |
| Investor Two |  |  | 240,000 | $300,000 | 240,000 | **6.8%** |

### Cap Table with a Series A Round of Financing

The second sheet allows you to create a cap table with both a Series A and Series B round. In both sheets, we provide a waterfall analysis so you can model exactly how much capital is returned to each shareholder and each class of stock under a variety of exit scenarios.

These sheets were designed with a fairly common capitalization structure in mind. The sheets support the following key features:

- Either one or two rounds of Series Preferred Stock
- Participating and Non-Participating Preferred Shares
- Liquidation Preferences
- Options, both Issued and Non-Issued
- Waterfall Analysis to model multiple exit scenarios

### Summary Cap Table

| Security Type | Outstanding Shares | Price per Share | Liquidation Preference | Percent Ownership |
|---|---|---|---|---|
| Common Shares | 2,200,000 | | | 66% |
| Issued Options | 140,000 | | | 4% |
| Series A Preferred Shares - Participating | 1,000,000 | $1.25 | $1,250,000 | 30% |
| Total Shares Outstanding | 3,340,000 | | | |

### Exit Proceeds

| | Price | Price | Price | Price |
|---|---|---|---|---|
| Purchase Price for the Company | $2,000,000 | $4,175,000 | $10,000,000 | $20,000,000 |

### Liquidation Preference Calculation

| | | | | |
|---|---|---|---|---|
| Series A Liquidation Preference | $1,250,000 | $1,250,000 | $1,250,000 | $1,250,000 |
| Remaining Proceeds | $750,000 | $2,925,000 | $8,750,000 | $18,750,000 |
| Proceeds per Common Share | $0.22 | $0.88 | $2.62 | $5.61 |
| Proceeds per Series A Share (as converted) | $0.22 | $0.88 | $2.62 | $5.61 |
| Total Proceeds per Series A Share | $1.47 | $2.13 | $3.87 | $6.86 |

### Returned Capital by Round

| | | | | |
|---|---|---|---|---|
| Common Shares | $494,012 | $1,926,647 | $5,763,473 | $12,350,299 |
| Options | $31,437 | $122,605 | $366,766 | $785,928 |
| Series A Preferred | $1,474,551 | $2,125,749 | $3,869,760 | $6,863,772 |
| Total Proceeds | $2,000,000 | $4,175,000 | $10,000,000 | $20,000,000 |
| Series A Return Multiple | 1.2 | 1.7 | 3.1 | 5.5 |

**Waterfall Analysis with a Series A Round of Financing**

It's also important to note that for the sake of simplicity and usability these sheets are NOT designed to support the following items commonly found in cap tables:

- More than two rounds of Series Preferred Stock
- Convertible Notes
- Dividends
- Warrants

So, if you are looking for a complete solution that will help you manage every aspect of your company's cap table, just do a Google search and you will find plenty of great products to purchase. In the meantime, try out these free Google sheets to help you build a well structured cap table along with a waterfall analysis for exit scenario modeling.

# Exit Planning Guide

As a director on an early stage company board, how do you deliver on your main responsibility as a board member - maximizing shareholder value? And, what do you do to make sure the CEO is doing her job in increasing the value of your investment in the company? And what good is the increase in value if it is not accompanied by sufficient liquidity to realize it? Those are very important questions that very few early stage company boards take the time and effort to ask early on when it is still possible to have the biggest impact.

The startup company IPO is a much rarer creature than it used to be, so most early stage companies return maximum value to their shareholders through some form of acquisition. Planning for such an exit is an ongoing responsibility for both the CEO and the board. With that challenge in mind, we put together a guide to help with this planning exercise. CEOs should use this guide as an approach or checklist to help stay on top of who their potential acquirers are and what the company's relationship is with each acquirer. And, furthermore, CEOs should use this guide as a way to update the board on at least an annual basis.

**What topics are covered in the exit planning guide for early stage companies?**

For each potential acquiring company, the guide asks the following questions:

- **Status:** This really goes to awareness.  What is the status of any discussions?  What do they know about our company? Who are the key people we met with? Describe the key relationships we have within this acquirer? Do we need to develop additional relationships?
- **Need:** Why would the acquirer want to buy our company? Are we a "must have" or a "nice to have"?
- **Value:** What do they value us for and what kind of valuation rubric might they use?  Are they buying us for our people, our technology, our product or our business? What might our company be worth to the acquirer? How will they determine the value - as a multiple of revenue or EBITDA; using a buy vs. build vs. partner analysis, or for some strategic reason like keeping us out of the hands of a competitor?
- **Milestones:** What milestones will we need to achieve before the acquirer will be interested?
- **Current Opportunities:** What opportunities do we have to work with the acquirer before an acquisition is made? What actions are we taking on these opportunities?
- **Appetite for Acquisition:** What acquisitions has this company made in the past few years? What price have they paid for these acquisitions?

By answering these questions with some level of detail, you will get a much better sense for what your company needs to accomplish before it's well positioned for an acquisition. Since putting all your eggs in one basket is not a great strategy, you will want to have a list of at least 5 acquiring companies and preferably more in the range of 10 to 15.

**What are some of the questions a potential acquirer will ask an early stage company?**

Once you reach the point where there is serious interest in acquiring your company, you will need to be prepared to answer some challenging questions. Some of these questions are specific to your company's growth plans, and we expect the CEO and board have been focused on answering these questions for quite some time.

- What are the key metrics you track to understand how your business is growing? How have those metrics been trending over the past year?
- What do you believe is the total addressable market for your business?
- Where do you see the greatest opportunities for growth in your business? What are you doing today to go after those opportunities?
- What companies do you see as your biggest competitors and what do you think differentiates your products from their products?
- How close to your annual plan have you been over the past 8 quarters? How confident are you in your projects for the upcoming 4 quarters?

Other questions will be specific to your willingness to be acquired. The buyer will want to understand your motivations and fit with their company. So be prepared with great answers to the following questions:

- What are your reasons for selling the company?
- What do you see as the most important synergies between our company and yours?
- After we complete the acquisition, what role will the CEO and her management team play in our company?

These two sets of questions are by no means complete. But, they are a starting point that will help you think about what questions are important for a potential buyer of your company. Start with these questions, add some of your own, and make sure the CEO can answer them all in a credible fashion.

| Company | Status | Need | Value |
|---|---|---|---|
| Name of potential acquiring company | What do they know about our company? Who are the key people we met with? Describe the key relationships we have within this acquirer. Do we need to develop additional relationships? | Why would the acquirer want to buy our company? Are we a "must have" or a "nice to have"? | Are they buying us for our people, our technology, our product or our business? What might our company be worth to the acquirer? How will they determine the value? |
| | | | |
| | | | |
| | | | |
| | | | |

| Company | Milestones | Current Opportunities | Appetite for Acquisitions |
|---|---|---|---|
| Name of potential acquiring company | What milestones will we need to achieve before the acquirer will be interested? | What opportunities do we have to work with the acquirer before an acquisition is made? What actions are we taking on these opportunities? | What acquisitions has this company made in the past few years? What price have they paid for these acquisitions? |
| | | | |
| | | | |
| | | | |
| | | | |